# LEWIS CARROLL

## Looking-Glass Letters

# LEWIS CARROLL

## Looking-Glass Letters

*Selected and introduced by*
*Thomas Hinde*

### RIZZOLI
NEW YORK

HALF-TITLE: 'The Scanty Meal', cartoon by Dodgson for *The Rectory Umbrella*, one of the magazines he produced as a boy to entertain his family.

First published in the United States of America in 1992 by
Rizzoli International Publications, Inc.
300 Park Avenue
New York
NY 10010
Copyright © Collins & Brown 1991

Introduction and commentary copyright © Thomas Hinde 1991

The Letters of C. L. Dodgson (Lewis Carroll) copyright © by The Executors of the C. L. Dodgson Estate 1979

The Diaries of C. L. Dodgson (Lewis Carroll) copyright by The Executors of the C. L. Dodgson Estate

Extracts taken from *The Letters of Lewis Carroll, Vols I and II*, edited by Morton Norton Cohen with the assistance of Roger Lancelyn Green, first published by Macmillan Publishers Limited in 1979, by kind permission of the editor and publisher.

Conceived, edited and designed by Collins & Brown

Published in Great Britain in 1991 by Collins & Brown Ltd, Mercury House, 195 Knightsbridge, London SW7 1RE

Printed and bound in Hong Kong

FRONTISPIECE: 'The Mad Hatter's Tea Party', illustration by John Tenniel for *Alice's Adventures in Wonderland*, subsequently coloured for the *The Nursery 'Alice'*.

TITLE PAGE: Detail of a rebus letter to Georgina Watson, 1869.

**Library of Congress Cataloging-in-Publication Data**

Carroll, Lewis, 1832–1898.
    [Letters. Selections]
    Looking-glass letters/Lewis Carroll ; selected and introduced by Thomas Hinde.
      p.   cm.
    "First published in Great Britain in 1991 by Collins & Brown Limited . . . London" — T.p. verso.
    Includes index.
    ISBN 0–8478–1470–X
    1. Carroll, Lewis, 1832–1898 — Correspondence. 2. Authors, English — 19th century — Correspondence. I. Hinde, Thomas, 1926– II. Title.
PR4612.A4 1992
828'809 — dc20
[B]
                                  91-53134
                                  CIP

10 9 8 7 6 5 4 3 2 1
First American Edition

# CONTENTS

# INTRODUCTION

QUEEN VICTORIA, IT was said, so enjoyed *Alice's Adventures in Wonderland* that she asked for Mr Lewis Carroll's next book. She received *Condensation of Determinants*, a learned mathematical treatise published by Lewis Carroll under his real name, Charles Dodgson. Though Dodgson eventually denied that anything of the sort had happened, the story encapsulates a picture of the author of *Alice's Adventures in Wonderland* and *Through the Looking-Glass* which is as common today as it was in the 1890s: that Lewis Carroll, alias Charles Dodgson, spent his whole life as a don at Christ Church, Oxford, writing dull books on mathematics and logic but, by some extraordinary and never repeated fluke, suddenly, in his thirties, produced his two *Alice* masterpieces.

The truth is very different; Dodgson's interests and activities were far wider than mathematics and logic, ranging from amateur conjuring and the invention of games to sketching and above all photography — at a time when a photographic plate had to be exposed wet and a photographer's subjects to keep still for forty-five seconds. In addition, his academic studies were by no means confined to abstract theorizing, but led him to make proposals on such diverse subjects as voting systems for parliamentary elections and knock-out sporting competitions which would ensure not only that the best player won but that the second best came second. Above all, the *Alice* books were no aberration but the high point of a lifetime of imaginative writing which began in his school days and remained his central preoccupation until he died.

Dodgson also wrote letters — thousands and thousands of them. He wrote to friends and acquaintances, he wrote to the papers, he wrote to his family, including his ten brothers and sisters, and he wrote to the little girls like Alice Liddell who became the focus of his

RIGHT: *Charles Lutwidge Dodgson, alias Lewis Carroll, a self-portrait, probably taken in his early years at Oxford.*

LEFT: *Dodgson's sitting-room at Christ Church, Oxford, where he spent the whole of his working life teaching mathematics.*

emotional life. A careful estimate based on his own register of letters sent shows that he wrote over 100,000 between the age of twenty-nine and his death. To this must be added the many that he wrote in earlier years. One day in 1892 he made a list of people who were waiting, some for five or ten years, for letters from him and found they numbered sixty. 'The proper definition of "Man,"' he once wrote, is 'an animal that writes letters.'

Towards the end of his life he published a short essay on letter writing, with his own twelve rules. The first began, '*Write legibly*. The average temper of the human race would be perceptibly sweetened, if everybody obeyed this Rule! . . .' The last read, 'When you take your letters to the Post, *carry them in your hand*. If you put them into your pocket, you will take a long country-walk — I speak from experience — passing the Post-Office *twice*, going and returning, and, when you get home again, will find them *still* in your pocket!' No rules could produce the sort of letters he himself wrote. At their most inspired they contain inventions and flights of fancy which are at least the equal of those in the *Alice* books. Not surprisingly, these are the ones he wrote, like the *Alice* books themselves, for the amusement of his many little friends.

From at least 1853, his third year at Oxford, till Christmas 1897, three weeks before he died, he also kept a diary. Stuart Collingwood, his nephew, had the use of all thirteen volumes of this when he wrote and published within a year of Carroll's death the first Lewis Carroll biography. But because no one realized that interest in Dodgson would grow rather than decline, the diaries were forgotten and became lost. When found again, falling out of a cardboard box in a cellar, four volumes were missing. Two of these, alas, covered vital periods of his relationship with Alice Liddell, and from them we have only Collingwood's quotations.

My aim in making this new selection of Dodgson's letters has been to tell the story of his life as fully as possible in his own words. I have therefore included among his charming letters to 'little friends' others which relate to his family life, his Oxford academic life, his dealings with publishers and his many other interests. To complete the story where the letters leave gaps I have here and there included extracts from the diary.

BELOW AND LEFT: *Looking-glass letter written by Dodgson to his little friend Edith Ball on 6 November 1893. He asks her which she would like best, 'a horse that draws you in a cab, or a lady that draws your picture, or a dentist, that draws your teeth, or a Mother, that draws you into her arms, to give you a kiss?'*

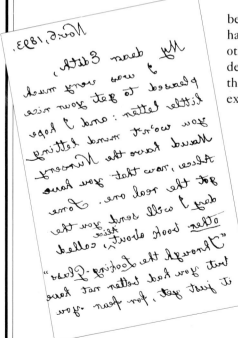

# Parson's Son

CHARLES LUTWIDGE DODGSON, born in January 1832, was the eldest son of a learned but poor Anglican clergyman, also named Charles and also a mathematician. Two sisters had been born earlier and five were to follow, as well as three brothers. None of the eleven Dodgson children died in infancy — remarkable in the mid-nineteenth century — and all but the last were born in the parsonage at Daresbury, a village fifteen miles north-east of Chester, deep in rural Cheshire.

As Perpetual Curate of Daresbury, Charles the father had an annual income of only about £190, and like many Anglican clergy of the time was forced to take pupils in order to survive. Charles the son was given his earliest lessons by his parents. According to a notebook kept by his mother, these consisted of private religious reading, religious reading 'with Mama', and private useful reading. At seven, for example, he read *Pilgrim's Progress*. He also read the improving tales of authors like Hannah More and Maria Edgeworth which he was later to parody. He was an intelligent boy and soon showed a particular interest in mathematics, but he was not considered outstanding either by his brothers and sisters or by his parents. In his father's opinion he was a 'steady, likely-to-do-good man, who in the long run may win the race.' The race which his father would have liked him to enter was the Church of England.

In 1884 the Daresbury parsonage was burned down, but the meadow where it stood is soon to become a shrine for the 7,000 visitors who come each year to see the village where the author of *Alice* was born. The outlines of the foundations have already been uncovered and they show that a parson of the time, besides being a cleric and teacher, must have been something of a smallholder. Around the courtyard with its central well there stood not only the

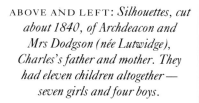

ABOVE AND LEFT: *Silhouettes, cut about 1840, of Archdeacon and Mrs Dodgson (née Lutwidge), Charles's father and mother. They had eleven children altogether — seven girls and four boys.*

LEFT: *Croft Rectory, the home to which Archdeacon Dodgson moved his family when his son, Charles, the future Lewis Carroll, was eleven. The move brought a rise in stipend, which enabled the Archdeacon to send his son to boarding school.*

LEFT: *Daresbury Parsonage, where Charles was born on 27 January 1832, and educated till he was twelve by his parents. All but one of his ten brothers and sisters were born here. It was burned down in 1884.*

L-shaped house containing seven bedrooms, but also a shed for four cows, stables for horses and a gig-house/laundry. It was in this sort of rustic environment that the Dodgson children grew up.

Charles was eleven when his father was at last given the much richer living of Croft, a small town in North Yorkshire, where his annual income was over a thousand pounds. The family moved to Croft in 1843, after a delay to enable Mrs Dodgson to have her tenth child. Charles the father now no longer needed to take pupils, and could afford to send his eldest boy away to school. So it was that on 1 August 1844, at the age of twelve, Charles the son became a boarder at Richmond School, a grammar school of about 120 boys and with a good reputation, situated ten miles south-west of Croft. It is his letters home that first begin to show the originality of his view of the world.

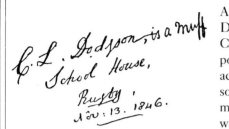

ABOVE: *Charles's signature in a school book, with the comment 'is a Muff' added in another hand, suggests that he was bullied. A 'gentle, intelligent and well-conducted boy' with no aptitude for games, Charles would have been a natural target.*

At Richmond he was taught by the headmaster, James Tate. Unlike Dodgson's parents, Tate formed a clear idea, after only one term, of Charles's potential. To the Dodgsons he wrote about their son, 'he possesses... a very uncommon share of genius... He is capable of acquirements and knowledge far beyond his years, while his reason is so clear and so jealous of error, that he will not rest satisfied without a most exact solution of whatever appears to him obscure...' Again it was mathematics at which Charles excelled.

Less than eighteen months later, on 27 January 1846, he was enrolled at Rugby. This ancient school had been somewhat civilized during the previous twenty years by Thomas Arnold, who had reduced the amount of flogging, caning and bullying. But, as *Tom Brown's Schooldays* proves, he had by no means entirely transformed the school, and a gentle, nervous boy like Charles, with a chronic stutter, whose interests were intellectual and who was no games player, was likely to suffer.

Suffer Charles did. In cold weather, in the big dormitory where he slept, he would have his blankets stolen and be left shivering all night. During the day he would spend 'an incalculable time writing out impositions — this last I consider one of the chief faults of Rugby School. I cannot say that I look back upon my life at a public school with any sensations of pleasure, or that any earthly considerations would induce me to go through my three years again.'

Teachers, however, once more praised his work. When he left, the headmaster wrote to his father, now Archdeacon Dodgson, 'His mathematical knowledge is great for his age.' He added that Charles's 'examination for the Divinity prize was one of the most creditable exhibitions I have ever seen.' Charles, it seemed, was developing as his father had hoped.

It was during his schooldays that he began to devise ways to amuse his brothers and sisters; indeed entertaining them undoubtedly satisfied that part of his nature which was later satisfied by entertaining his little girl friends. The amusements mainly took the form of private magazines. To some of these the whole family was

ABOVE: *Charles's father, himself a mathematician, valued learning highly and was pleased to hear good reports of his son's progress. 'You may fairly anticipate for him a bright career,' wrote James Tate, Charles's headmaster at Richmond Grammar School.*

meant to contribute, but they were mostly the work of Charles alone, who signed himself with various combinations of initials. In them appeared his earliest surviving poems, parodies and humorous tales.

The five issues of the first, *Useful and Instructive Poetry*, included limericks (eleven years before Edward Lear, in 1846, made the form famous) and other nonsense verse — 'The Headstrong Man', for example, the story of a cantankerous fellow who tumbles from a wall and clearly an early version of his 'Humpty Dumpty'.

*The Rectory Magazine* came soon afterwards and had nine issues. By this time Charles was probably about fifteen and his contributions were more mature. They included a serial story entitled 'Crumble

LEFT AND RIGHT: *From the age of thirteen, Charles was a keen illustrator. He kept a book of humorous ideas and cartoons, and many of his sketches were later coloured in by his brothers and sisters (left). The Rectory Umbrella was the most precocious of the family magazines he edited (and largely wrote and illustrated) for his brothers and sisters. In a parody of Macaulay's 'Horatius' written for the magazine, called 'Lays of Sorrow No. 2', Wilfred Dodgson gallantly helps his brother Skeffington to master a difficult donkey (far right). The feat takes place at Croft Rectory, where a great crowd gathers to watch (near right).*

*The deceitfull coachman*

Castle' in which two of the characters are early versions of Uggug and Uggug's mother who later appeared in his last children's book, *Sylvie and Bruno*. *The Comet* came next, then *The Rosebud*, *The Star* and *The Will-O-the-Wisp*, this last triangular in format. About *The Comet*, Charles later wrote:

> When the Comet next I started
>   They grew lazy as a drone.
> Gradually all departed
>   Leaving me to write alone.

Finally came *The Rectory Umbrella*, which Charles, now about eighteen, also wrote alone. This included a poem inspired by Macaulay's 'Horatius' which showed that his gift for parody was by now fully developed. 'Lay of Sorrow No. 2' told how his brother Wilfred Longley (disguised as 'Ulfrid Longbow'), helped another brother, Skeffington (called 'the knight'), to ride a donkey and, like Horatius, was properly rewarded:

> They gave him bread and butter,
>   That was of public right,
> As much as four strong rabbits,
>   Could munch from morn till night.
> For he'd done a deed of daring,
>   And faced that savage steed,
> And therefore cups of coffee sweet,
> And everything that was a treat,
>   Were but his right and meed.

Of the other family entertainments Charles devised at Croft Rectory, one was a railway game to be played in the garden, the rules of which began, 'All passengers when upset are requested to lie still until picked up — as it is requested that at least three trains should go over them, to entitle them to the attention of the doctor and assistants.'

Another was a marionette theatre, for which he wrote his own plays, including an Italian-style opera entitled *La Guida di Bragia* — an approximation for *Bradshaw's Guide* — in which two of the characters, Mooney and Spooney, were prototypes of Tweedledum and Tweed-ledee in *Through the Looking-Glass*. Railways were again the setting — they were only about twenty years old — and the arias included a passenger's parody of 'Auld Lang Syne'.

> Should all my luggage be forgot
> And never come to hand
> I'll never quit this fatal spot
> But perish where I stand.

---

*Charles Dodgson's first surviving letter was written to his nurse at home at the family parsonage at Daresbury, probably in 1837 when he was five. Marke, which has not been identified, was a place he was probably visiting with his father.*

My dear Bun,
    I love you very much, and tend you a kitt from little Charlie with the horn of hair. I'd like to give you a kitt, but I tan't, betause I'm at Marke. What a long letter I've written. I'm twite tired.

My dear Bun,
    I love you very much
& tend you a kitt from little
Charlie with the horn of hair.
I'd like to give you a kitt, but I
tan't, betause I'm at Marke. What
a long letter I've written. I'm twite
tired.

LEFT: *Charles wrote this, his first surviving letter, to his nurse at home when he was about five and probably away from home with his father. On the back an adult wrote, 'For dear kind Bun from little Charly.'*

◆

*Charles had just arrived as a boarder at Richmond when he wrote*
*home to his two elder sisters, Frances and Elizabeth.*

### RICHMOND SCHOOL, YORKSHIRE
### 5 AUGUST 1844

My dear Fanny and Memy,

    I hope you are all getting on well . . . The boys I think that I like the best, are Harry Austin, and all the Tates [sons of the headmaster] of which there are 7 besides a little girl who came down to dinner the first day, but not since . . .

LEFT: *Dodgson's photograph of his seven sisters, two older (Frances and Elizabeth), five younger (Caroline, Mary, Louisa, Margaret and Henrietta), taken in the garden at Croft Rectory.*

The boys have played two tricks upon me which were these — they first proposed to play at 'King of the cobblers' and asked me if I would be king, to which I agreed, then they made me sit down and sat (on the ground) in a circle round me, and told me to say 'Go to work' which I said and they immediately began kicking me and knocking on all sides. The next game they proposed was 'Peter, the red lion,' and they made a mark on a tombstone (for we were playing in the church-yard) and one of the boys walked with his eyes shut, holding out his finger, trying to touch the mark, then a little boy came forward to lead the rest and led a good many very near the mark; at last it was my turn, they told me to shut my eyes well, and the next minute I had my finger in the mouth of one of the boys, who had stood (I believe) *before* the tombstone with his mouth open . . .

I have had 3 misfortunes in my clothes etc., 1st I cannot find my tooth brush, so that I have not brushed my teeth for 3 or 4 days, 2nd I cannot find my blotting paper, and 3rd I have no shoe horn. The chief games are, foot-ball, wrestling, leap frog, and fighting. Excuse bad writing.

Your affectionate brother,
Charles

RIGHT: *Contemporary painting by George Pyne of Rugby School, one of the seven 'Great Schools' of England. Thomas Arnold had been headmaster from 1828 to 1840, and Charles went there six years later. He did not like it. On visiting another school in March 1857, and finding it fitted out with individual bedrooms, Dodgson recorded in his diary that if he too 'could have been secure from annoyance at night, the hardships of the daily life would have been comparative trifles to bear.'*

◆

*Charles's first surviving letter from his second school, Rugby, was to his sister, Elizabeth. The co-author of* A Greek-English Lexicon, *which Charles asks permission to get, was Henry Liddell. As Dean of Christ Church, Liddell was to become Charles's life-long employer. His second daughter, Alice Liddell, was to be the major inspiration of Dodgson's life.*

SCHOOL HOUSE, RUGBY
9 OCTOBER 1848

Dearest Elizabeth,

Thank you for your letter . . . I have *not* got any warm gloves yet but must do so soon. Now I think of it, I should like 10s. of my own money to be sent: I can settle about the gloves afterward. . .

RIGHT AND OPPOSITE:
*Dodgson's drawings for the family magazine* The Rectory Umbrella. *His poem 'Lays of Sorrow No. 1' (right) tells of a fearless mother hen addicted to infanticide. 'Ye Fatalle Cheyse' (opposite) is a mock ballad, recounting a fox hunt. The hounds chase their prey into a sinister cave, where a monster proceeds to eat them. The king, their master, who goes to rescue them, only just escapes a similar fate.*

The report is certainly a delightful one: *I* cannot account for it; I hope there is no mistake. As to the difference between Walker and myself (Papa seems satisfied about Harrison) it must be remembered that he is in the 6th and has hitherto been considered the best mathematician in the school . . .

There are some books I should like to have leave to get: these are ~~Butler's Ancient Atlas~~ (on 2nd thoughts not yet). Liddell and Scott's Larger *Greek-English Lexicon*. Mr Price quite despises the little one and says it is only fit for my younger brothers. It is hardly any use in Demosthenes . . .

With best love to all I remain —

Your most affectionate brother,
Charles

✦

*To his sister Elizabeth*

### SCHOOL HOUSE, RUGBY
### 24 MAY 1849

Dearest Elizabeth,

. . . Thanks for the two letters received yesterday, also for the promise of the box, about which I wish to offer one more hint and that is, please do *not* send me one of Mrs Pattinson's seed loaf cakes, they are so light that they are gone directly and are neither worth the carriage nor the money . . .

Yesterday evening I was walking out with a friend of mine who attends as mathematical pupil Mr Smythies, the second mathematical master, we went up to Mr Smythies' house, as he wanted to speak to him, and he asked us to stop and have a glass of wine and some figs. He seems as devoted to his duty as Mr Mayor, and asked me with a smile of delight, 'Well, Dodgson, I suppose you're getting well on with your mathematics?' He is very clever at them though not equal to Mr Mayor, as indeed very few men are, Papa excepted . . .

I have got a new hat, which I suppose Papa will not object to, as my old one was getting very shabby; which I have had ever since the

beginning of last holidays. I have also got a pair of gloves, as I found I had not *one* pair of summer gloves, as I thought I had . . .

Will my room be ready for me when I come home? And has it got any more 'visitors'? Have you been many walks with Aunt and Cousin Smedley? And how long are they going to stay with you? Are my two pictures of cricketing framed yet? When is Papa going to the Ordination? And when to the Durham examination? Has Fanny yet finished Alison's *Europe*? Have you finished your Hutchinson? Are the mats finished? Is Skeffington's ship finished? Have you left off fires yet? Have you begun the evening walks in the garden? Does Skeffington ride Henderson's donkey much now? Has Fanny found any new flowers? Have you got any new babies to nurse? Mary any new pictures to paint? Has Mr Stamper given up the ball room yet? Will you tell me whose and when the birthdays in next month are? Will you condense all these questions into one or answer each separately? Lastly, Do you believe that I subscribe myself your

Affectionate Brother, sincerely or not? Is this letter long enough?

<sup>(1)</sup> 'drawn <sup>(2)</sup> bystanders <sup>(3)</sup> heavy. <sup>(4)</sup> sounds <sup>(5)</sup> fetched <sup>(6)</sup> pull <sup>(7)</sup> haul. <sup>(8)</sup> all.

# Oxford Academic

LEFT: *Tom Tower, Christ Church Oxford, which Dodgson entered as a mathematics student in 1850, aged eighteen, and where he was awarded a Studentship (equivalent to a Fellowship at other colleges), at the end of 1852. After gaining a first-class degree, he became a permanent member of the college common room, and spent the rest of his life there, unmarried, as a deacon and mathematics don.*

IN 1850 CHARLES DODGSON matriculated at Christ Church, Oxford, his father's old college. The story of his life during the next five years is one of steady academic progress, of scholarships won, exams passed and eventually, after a series of promotions, of a college Mastership.

Because accommodation was in short supply at Christ Church, he did not in fact come to live at Oxford until January the following year. Two days afterwards he heard that his mother had died. She had been, according to a friend, 'one of the sweetest and gentlest women that ever lived.' It must have been a considerable shock to Dodgson that she should die so unexpectedly, aged only forty-seven, and for some while he wrote on the customary black-edged mourning paper.

That November he won a £20 scholarship, and the following year, in Moderations, was awarded a first class in mathematics and a second class in classics. The same Christmas he was given a Studentship, the equivalent of a Fellowship at other colleges, worth £25 a year and tenable for life, provided he progressed towards ordination in the Church and did not marry. Although two years later he gained only a third class in philosophy and history, he soon afterwards (October 1854) won a first class in mathematics finals. He now began to supplement his income by taking pupils. Finally in October 1855 he was 'made Master and tutor in Christ Church', bringing his income to over £300 a year.

During these five years, however, he had not spent the whole of his time in academic studies. Soon after he arrived, he went with a friend to listen to the Oxford assizes. They were frustrated — the assize had already ended — but the incident suggests that he enjoyed attending law courts; the court scene in *Alice's Adventures in Wonderland* shows his knowledge of the law's bizarre rituals.

ABOVE: *Portrait of Dodgson, aged about twenty-five, attributed to his friend and colleague, Reginald Southey. It was with Southey that he first went photographing in the gardens of the Deanery at Christ Church, where he met Alice Liddell, the Dean's daughter*

The same year (1851) he went to London to see the Great Exhibition in the Crystal Palace. More significantly, while visiting London during the following long vacation he called on his mother's brother, Skeffington Lutwidge, a bachelor barrister, who shared his interest in gadgets and inventions. Uncle Skeffington showed his nephew a microscope, a telescope stand, a lathe and a refrigerator.

Dodgson also continued to write, several of his pieces being published in *The Comic Times* — a short-lived magazine founded in 1855. The same year, he began to compile a scrapbook of his best published and unpublished writings, called *Mischmasch*. It included a four-line verse of particular interest entitled 'Stanza of Anglo-Saxon Poetry'. This was to become the first verse of the most famous of his nonsense poems, 'Jabberwocky'.

It was only at the end of this period that two things happened which were to have the greatest influence on his life. One was the arrival at Christ Church of the new Dean, Henry Liddell, the other was his decision to take up photography. Had either of these not occurred the *Alice* books could never have been written, for Alice was the Dean's daughter, and it was through photography that he got to know her.

Though Liddell was now well known for his *A Greek-English Lexicon*, which he compiled with Robert Scott, Master of Balliol, he was still only forty-four, and young to become Dean. He had previously been headmaster of Westminster School, and was regarded as something of a reformer. He was also a talented draughtsman and a critic, described by Ruskin as 'the only man in Oxford among the Masters of my day who knew anything about art.' At the time of his appointment he had a son, Harry, and three daughters: Lorina Charlotte, Alice and Edith. Alice was three years old.

Dodgson became interested in photography through a Christ Church friend, Reginald Southey, and his uncle Skeffington. He and Skeffington took photographs around Croft during the long vacation of 1855. The following March, Dodgson went to London and spent £15 on a camera of his own.

ABOVE: *Alice Liddell, photographed by Dodgson. He first met the Liddell family in 1856, going to the Oxford boat races. Alice was to become the muse of the Alice books and the major inspiration of Dodgson's life.*

At about the same time (August 1855), while staying at Whitburn, near Sunderland, he made his first social contact with a member of the Liddell family. She was the Dean's niece, Frederika Liddell, a little girl who charmed him. Within two days he had sketched her, and soon afterwards acted with her at a charade party. 'One of the nicest children I have ever seen,' he wrote, 'as well as the prettiest; dear, sweet, pretty little Frederika.' Something about Liddells as children seems to have particularly delighted Dodgson.

He first encountered Dean Liddell himself and his family the following February when they were on the same train going to the Oxford boat races. But it was only two months later, when he and his friend Southey went to the Deanery garden to photograph the cathedral, that he and Alice met properly for the first time. Finding the Dean's children there, he tried to arrange them as a foreground for the picture; this was not a success as they 'were not patient sitters'.

Over six years passed before *Alice* the story was first told. Meanwhile Dodgson formed an increasingly close friendship with Alice the child, and with her brother and sisters. At first he achieved

25

this by coming to the Deanery to take their photographs, telling them stories to induce them to keep still. The Dean and his wife seemed pleased. But already during that autumn of 1856 Mrs Liddell told him to take no more photographs until she could assemble a complete family group. 'This may be a hint that I have intruded on the premises long enough,' Dodgson wrote in his diary.

As an alternative, he began to teach mathematics to Alice's older brother, Harry, but again Mrs Liddell objected, saying that Mr Dodgson would not have sufficient time. Fortunately for Dodgson, the Liddell parents spent the rest of that winter abroad and Miss Prickett, the governess they left in charge ('Pricks' to the children) let him visit them as often as he liked. When the Dean and his wife returned he was allowed to continue to befriend them, and it became his custom to take them on boating expeditions up or down the Thames four or five times each summer.

Dodgson continued during these six years to make progress along the two paths which his father had hoped he would follow: mathematics and the Church. In 1860 he published his first two mathematical textbooks; by the following February he had completed another and partly written four more. And he spent the years from 1858 onwards preparing himself for Holy Orders. He attended Cuddlesdon Theological College near Oxford, and here, in December 1861, he was ordained as a deacon. There is no doubt that he intended to become a priest — in 1865, for example, he set himself a reading list which included sections of the Bible and commentators like Hooker. But a deacon he was to remain for the rest of his life.

Several reasons for this have been suggested. Certainly his stammer made preaching difficult for him; until twenty-three years old he never preached at all and increasingly he used this as his own explanation. In addition, as a logician, he must have had more religious doubts than most Christians. He once wrote about a sermon at Eastbourne that the preacher had 'advanced the astonishing argument "We believe that the Bible is true, because our Holy Mother, the Church, tells us it is." I pity that unfortunate clergyman,'

ABOVE: *Skeffington Lutwidge (Dodgson's mother's brother) was his favourite uncle. They were both fascinated by scientific gadgetry, and it was Skeffington who introduced him to photography.*

RIGHT: *The Great Exhibition, staged in the Crystal Palace created specially for it in Hyde Park, was the London sensation of 1851. Dodgson made a special journey down from Oxford to see it and was duly impressed by the exciting examples of modern engineering on display — especially the Crystal Fountain, and curiosities such as a treeful of mechanical birds.*

he continued, 'if he is ever bold enough to enter any Young Men's Debating Club.' Perhaps he was also troubled by his keen interest in the theatre, at a time when Wilberforce, Bishop of Oxford, considered that 'resolution to attend theatres or operas was an absolute disqualification for Holy Orders.' But it seems more likely that what he suffered from most was a sense of his general unworthiness. By 1867 he felt that even to have become a deacon was 'almost a desecration with my undisciplined and worldly affections.'

In these six years he also continued to pursue his main private interest: writing. When *The Comic Times* collapsed, its staff started a new magazine, *The Train*, and he contributed a total of eight pieces to this. At first he signed himself BB, initials he had often used before, but he was soon asked by the editor, Edmund Yates, to choose a full pseudonym. He thought of Dares, derived from his birthplace, Daresbury, but eventually sent Yates four other suggestions: Edgar Cuthwellis, Edgar U. C. Westhall, Louis Carroll and Lewis Carroll. Yates chose the fourth. Dodgson had invented it by Latinizing and reversing his first two names: Lutwidge = Ludovicus = Lewis; Charles = Carolus = Carroll. In March 1856 Lewis Carroll appeared for the first time as the author of a poem, 'Solitude'. The Crimean War had just ended and the poem — a serious one — was about Florence Nightingale.

He also wrote poems for the privately published *College Rhymes*, and in 1860 he combined his two interests by writing a comic article for the *South Shields Amateur Magazine* called 'A Photographer's Day Out'. Photography had meanwhile led him in more interesting directions. While at Croft in August 1857 he took portraits of Agnes Grace Weld, Tennyson's wife's small niece, dressed as Little Red Riding Hood. When Tennyson saw a copy and pronounced it 'indeed a gem', Dodgson found the courage to go to Tent Lodge near Coniston in the Lake District where the Tennysons were staying, and call on them. He was kindly received by Mrs Tennyson and began to edge his way towards persuading the great man to sit for him. He was now in the habit of taking an album of prints around with him to show

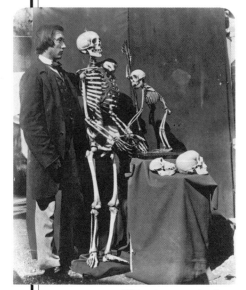

ABOVE: *This photograph of Reginald Southey, a medical student, with a range of ape and monkey skeletons (topical, since Darwin's theories of evolution were being fiercely debated at the time) was taken by Dodgson. Of all the photographs Dodgson showed Tennyson, the anatomical ones especially intrigued him.*

friends, and when Tennyson saw this Dodgson reported that some of them 'called out a good deal of fun on Mr Tennyson's part . . . The anatomical photographs intrigued him, and especially a group of human skeletons and monkey,' which he had taken at Oxford. Eventually he got his wish — a sitting with Tennyson.

Dodgson's pursuit of Tennyson now took the curious form of his editing *An Index to In Memorium*. This was compiled by his sisters and consisted of 3,000 references to the poem which Tennyson had written to commemorate his great friend, Arthur Hallam. In May 1859 and again in April 1862 he also went to the Isle of Wight to stay at Freshwater, where the poet lived. The first visit was a success, but during most of the second Tennyson was, typically, preoccupied, though he did find time to admire a photograph of Alice Liddell dressed as a beggar-child. Dodgson was more successful with the two Tennyson children, Hallam and Lionel, teaching them to play the Dodgson family game of 'elephant-hunters', and organizing them, together with other local children, all dressed in uniform, 'to represent the battle of Waterloo.'

Two of these other children were those of Julia Margaret Cameron, the most celebrated of Tennyson's pursuers, and one of the most remarkable photographers of the time. At Freshwater, Dodgson photographed Mrs Cameron and her children, and the Tennysons' house and servants, but was not granted another sitting with Tennyson himself.

ABOVE: *View of Oxford from across the meadows, showing Tom Tower (left) and Christ Church Cathedral.*

ABOVE: *Dodgson's photograph of Tennyson's wife's niece, Agnes Grace Weld, dressed as Little Red Riding Hood, taken at Croft in 1857. Tennyson called it 'indeed a gem', and subsequently let Dodgson take his photograph.*

◆

*From Oxford Dodgson reported regularly to his family on student life. Two months after taking up residence there he wrote to his sister Mary.*

CHRIST CHURCH, OXFORD
6 MARCH 1851

Dearest Mary,

Many very happy returns of your birthday . . . I am not so anxious as usual to begin my personal history, as the first thing I have to record is a very sad incident, namely my missing morning chapel; before

however you condemn me, you must hear how accidental it was. For some days now I have been in the habit of — I will not say getting up, but of being called at ¼ past 6, and generally managing to be down soon after 7. In the present instance I had been up the night before till about ½ past 12, and consequently when I was called I fell asleep again, and was thunderstruck to find on waking that it was 10 minutes past 8 . . .

This afternoon I was sitting in my room when I heard a sudden shrieking of dogs, as if fighting: I rushed to the window, but the fight, if any, was over, having lasted for about the space of 3 seconds, and every thing and every body was flying from the scene of combat: six dogs went headlong down the steps, which lead into the quad, yelling at the very top of their voices; six sticks came flying after them, and after that came their six masters, all running their hardest, and all in different directions. For a little time none of the dogs knew which way to go, so they went darting about, tumbling over each other, screaming, and getting hit by the sticks, and their masters did the same only they screamed in a different manner: at last 3 dogs got away and ran straight home, screaming as they went, 2 others were hunted up and down the quad by their masters, I suppose with the intention of beating them, but were never sufficiently caught for that purpose, and the sixth went home with its master . . .

In routing over my wardrobe the other day I discovered a curious and far from satisfactory circumstance, namely that I have left all my silk neck handkerchiefs at home. The only things of the kind I possess here are the handkerchief I now have on, and a black satin tie for the evening. Will you hunt them up at Croft and send them: if you cannot find them I will look for them again but I do not think they are here.

I think this is one of the most magnificently long letters I have ever written.

With best love to all, I remain

Your very affectionate Brother,
Charles Lutwidge Dodgson

ABOVE: *An Oxford student signing his name in the Matriculation Book. Dodgson matriculated at Oxford in 1850 but, because the college was so crowded, only came into residence in 1851.*

*To his sister Elizabeth*

CHRIST CHURCH, OXFORD
9 DECEMBER 1852

Dearest Elizabeth,

You shall have the announcement of the last piece of good fortune this wonderful term has had in store for me, that is, *a 1st class in Mathematics*. Whether I shall add to this any honours at collections I cannot at present say, but I should think it very unlikely, as I have only today to get up the work in The Acts of the Apostles, 2 Greek Plays, and the Satires of Horace and I feel myself almost totally unable to read at all: I am beginning to suffer from the reaction of reading for Moderations . . .

I am getting quite tired of being congratulated on various subjects: there seems to be no end of it. If I had shot the Dean, I could hardly have had more said about it . . .

Best love to all

Your very affectionate Brother,
Charles L. Dodgson

◆

*To his sister Mary*

### CHRIST CHURCH, OXFORD
### 13 DECEMBER 1854

My dear Sister,

Enclosed you will find a list, which I expect you to rejoice over considerably: it will take me more than a day to believe it, I expect — I feel at present very like a child with a new toy, but I daresay I shall be tired of it soon, and wish to be Pope of Rome next. Those in the list who were of the Whitby party are, Fowler, Ranken, Almond, and Wingfield. I have just given my Scout a bottle of wine to drink to my First. We shall be made Bachelors on Monday: I *think* I may be able to come home on the Tuesday, but I am not sure yet, and will write again about it. If you have not yet sent the London order will you get *The Life of R. Haydon* for me? That is, unless it happens to be in the Ripon Library. I hope that Papa did not conclude it was a 2nd by not hearing on Wednesday morning. I have just been to Mr Price to see how I did in the papers, and the result will I hope be gratifying to you. The following were the sums total of the marks for each in the 1st class, as nearly as I can remember:

Dodgson ........................ 279
Bosanquet ....................... 261
Cookson ......................... 254
Fowler .......................... 225
Ranken .......................... 213

He also said he never remembered so good a set of men in. All this is very satisfactory. I must also add (this is a very boastful letter) that I ought to get the Senior Scholarship next term.

Your very affectionate Brother,
Charles L. Dodgson

ABOVE: *Christ Church undergraduates photographed by Dodgson (from left to right, Twis, Lane and Williams).*

*On the last day of January 1855 Dodgson described to his sister
Henrietta and his brother Edwin his first experience of
Oxford tutoring.*

### CHRIST CHURCH, OXFORD
### 31 JANUARY 1855

My dear Henrietta,

My dear Edwin,

My one pupil has begun his work with me, and I will give you a description how the lecture is conducted. It is the most important point, you know, that the tutor should be *dignified*, and at a distance from the pupil, and that the pupil should be as much as possible *degraded* — otherwise you know, they are not humble enough. So I sit at the further end of the room; outside the door (*which is shut*) sits the scout; outside the outer door (*also shut*) sits the sub-scout; half-way down stairs sits the sub-sub-scout; and down in the yard sits the *pupil*.

The questions are shouted from one to the other, and the answers come back in the same way — it is rather confusing till you are well used to it. The lecture goes on, something like this.

*Tutor* 'What is twice three?'

*Scout* 'What's a rice tree?'

*Sub-Scout* 'When is ice free?'

*Sub-sub-Scout* 'What's a nice fee?'

*Pupil* (timidly) 'Half a guinea!'

*Sub-sub-Scout* 'Can't forge any!'

*Sub-Scout* 'Ho for Jinny!'

*Scout* 'Don't be a ninny!'

*Tutor* (looks offended, but tries another question)
'Divide a hundred by twelve!'

*Scout* 'Provide wonderful bells!'

*Sub-Scout* 'Go ride under it yourself.'

*Sub-sub-Scout* 'Deride the dunder-headed elf!'

*Pupil* (surprised) 'Who do you mean?'

ABOVE: *Dodgson's own idea of
what he looked like when lecturing.
Part of his apprehension must have
stemmed from his incurable
stammer, 'yet still I think there's
something grand in the expression of
the brow and in the action
of the hand.'*

*Sub-sub-Scout* 'Doings between!'
*Sub-Scout* 'Blue is the screen!'
*Scout* 'Soup-tureen!'

And so the lecture proceeds.
    Such is Life — from

Your most affectionate brother,
Charles L. Dodgson

◆

*When Queen Victoria visited Oxford on 12 December 1860 Dodgson*
*described the event to his family.*

### CHRIST CHURCH, OXFORD
#### 18 DECEMBER 1860

. . . She was only a minute or two in the Hall, during which the Dean pointed out some of the chief pictures, and presented the Sub-dean. With her were Prince Albert, Princess Alice, Prince of Wales, Prince Alfred, and suite. I had never seen her so near before, nor on her feet, and was shocked to find how short, not to say dumpy, and with all loyalty be it spoken, how *plain* she is . . .

You will be sorry to hear that I have failed, finally and completely, in getting H. R. H. to sit for his photograph. I will give you the history of my proceedings in the matter, which will show you that I did not fail for want of asking, and that, if ever impudence and importunity deserved to succeed, I did . . .

Last Wednesday we were asked to an evening party at the Deanery to meet the Prince. I need not say that I got hold of General Bruce, and claimed the fulfilment of his promise to introduce me, which he most readily did. The Prince shook hands very graciously, and I began by apologising for having been so troublesome about the photograph. He looked perhaps a *little* ashamed of himself, and said something about the weather being unfavourable. I asked him if the Americans had victimised him much as a sitter, and he said 'yes, but they had not succeeded well,' and we talked for 2 or 3 minutes about

ABOVE: *Queen Victoria, who visited Oxford in 1860. This portrait shows her in a pose which fully justifies Dodgson's blunt appraisal of her appearance.*

ABOVE: *Mrs Liddell. She eventually became concerned about the nature of Dodgson's friendship with her daughter and placed restrictions on it.*

photographs, my pictures of the Liddells, and the *tableaux vivants* which were to form the entertainment of the evening. When I say 'we,' it should rather be, that *I* talked to *him*, for he was anything but suggestive of conversation himself, seeming rather shy and silent . . .

I here conclude one of the largest letters I have written for some time. Make the most of it.

Your very affectionate brother,
Charles L. Dodgson

---

*To his sister Mary*

CHRIST CHURCH, OXFORD
20 FEBRUARY 1861

My dear Mary,

I am quite ashamed of having been silent so long, and do *not* think that I deserved so long a letter ... I write now, partly because I have an hour without a lecture ...

As you ask about my mathematical books I will give you a list of my 'Works.'

1. Syllabus, etc., etc. (done)
2. Notes on Euclid (done)
3. Ditto on Algebra (done — will be out this week, I hope)
4. Cycle of examples, Pure Mathematics (about ⅓ done)
5. Collection of formulae (½ done)
6. Collection of Symbols (begun)
7. Algebraical Geometry in 4 vols. (about ¼ of Vol. I done).

Doesn't it look grand?

I congratulate you on having learnt to spell 'reckon.' I had noticed the former version. Not much going on here but the usual botheration of lectures. My small friends the Liddells are all in the measles just now. I met them yesterday. Alice had been pronounced as commencing, and looked *awfully* melancholy — it was almost impossible to make her smile. I need not say I have given them a copy

ABOVE: *Alice's father, the Dean of Christ Church, Oxford. The Deanery gardens were the scene of many entertaining games of croquet between Dodgson and the young Liddell girls. He also began to take the girls on boating trips — the seeds of the* Alice *stories were being sown.*

RIGHT: *Dodgson's photograph of Alice Liddell (seated and reading) with two of her four sisters, Lorina (standing) and Edith, who most closely resembled Dodgson's physical conception of the fictional 'Alice', as depicted in his own drawings and sketches.*

of *College Rhymes* — they say the 'Sea-dirge' is 'not true' — rather a sweeping condemnation.

This must do for the present.

Your very affectionate brother,
Charles L. Dodgson

◆

*During vacations Dodgson would sometimes return to Croft, or visit nearby seaside resorts. From Whitby, where he was one of Professor Price's mathematical reading party, he wrote to his sister Mary.*

**5 EAST TERRACE, WHITBY**
**23 AUGUST 1834**

My dear Mary,

I have just been out to buy some note-paper, and am returned breathless and exhausted: there is a strong wind blowing off shore, and threatening to carry Whitby and contents into the sea. There is sand and sharp shingle flying in the air, that acts on the face like the smart cut of a whip, and here and there the painful sight of an old lady being whirled round a corner in a paroxysm of dust and despair . . .

ABOVE: *Statue of the Amazon and Tiger at the Great Exhibition of 1851, much admired by Dodgson for its realism.*

Yesterday was the school-feast, at which the inhabitants and visitors were invited to attend: it was given in the grounds near the Abbey ... Mr Price and one of our men joined in carrying currant-bread. As fast as a supply of the latter came round, the boys stuffed it into their pockets, and waited for the next basket. Some means ought to have been taken to prevent this, though I can't say I could have suggested any. Now comes the shocking part; in the middle of the feast down came the rain in torrents, and nothing was to be seen but flight, uproar, and confusion. All the visitors went home, I among others: the man who helped in the currant-bread stayed through the shower, and related to us the rest of the proceedings. The feast went on when the sky cleared; I suppose they did not mind soaked bread and cold tea. When it was over, Mr Keane told them all to shut their eyes, that he might say grace: after a short silence he said, 'I see one boy with his eyes quite wide open': an unfortunate speech, which raised a general laugh ...

I am doing Integral Calculus with him [Professor Price] now, and getting on very swimmingly. This is a much longer letter than I expected to write. I hope you will excuse their coming seldom, on account of their great length when they do come.

Best love to all.

Your very affectionate Brother,
Charles L. Dodgson

P.S. A mother and child have just passed, the mother *holding the child's head* as it walks; I suppose to prevent its being blown off! ...

RIGHT: *The Yorkshire resort of Whitby, where Dodgson went with Professor Price's reading party in 1854, attending a school-feast near the Abbey (top right), and where, according to a fellow student, he would 'sit on a rock on the beach, telling stories to a circle of eager young listeners of both sexes.'*

---

*On other occasions Dodgson would go to London. Here, in July 1851, he visited the Great Exhibition, and reported to his sister Elizabeth.*

### SPRING GARDENS, LONDON
#### 5 JULY 1851

Dearest Elizabeth,

... It looks like a sort of fairyland. As far as you can look in any direction, you see nothing but pillars hung about with shawls, carpets,

etc., with long avenues of statues, fountains, canopies, etc., etc., etc. The first thing to be seen on entering is the Crystal Fountain, a most elegant one about 30 feet high at a rough guess, composed entirely of glass and pouring down jets of water from basin to basin: this is in the middle of the centre nave and from it you can look down to either end, and up both transepts. The centre of the nave mostly consists of a long line of colossal statues, some most magnificent. The one considered the finest, I believe, is the Amazon and Tiger. She is sitting on horseback, and a tiger has fastened on the neck of the horse in front. You have to go to one side to see her face, and the other to see the horse's. The horse's face is really wonderful, expressing terror and pain so exactly, that you almost expect to hear it scream. She is leaning back to strike at the tiger with a spear, and her expression is of steady determination with the least fear. A pair of statues of a dog and child struck me as being exceedingly good. In one the child is being attacked by a serpent, and the dog standing over to defend it. The child is crying with fear, and making I think an exceedingly ugly face. In the other the dog has conquered: the body of the serpent is lying at one side, and the head, *most thoroughly* bitten off, at the other. The dog seems to have quite chewed the neck of the serpent to make sure. The child is leaning over and playing with the dog, which is *really* smiling with pleasure and satisfaction . . .

There are some very ingenious pieces of mechanism. A tree (in the French Compartment) with birds chirping and hopping from branch to branch exactly like life. The bird jumps across, turns round on the other branch, settles its head and neck, and then in a few moments jumps back again. A bird standing at the foot of the tree trying to eat a beetle is rather a failure (I am blotting dreadfully); the beetle is lying very conveniently before it, but it never succeeds in getting its head more than a quarter of an inch down, and that in uncomfortable little jerks, as if it was choking . . .

Your very affectionate Brother,
Charles

ABOVE: *Miss Prickett, governess to Alice Liddell and her sisters. When Dean and Mrs Liddell went abroad, 'Pricks' was left in charge, and allowed Dodgson free access to the children. She later ran Oxford's Mitre Hotel.*

ABOVE: *Dodgson's sketch of 'the ugliest boy I ever saw', made at a concert at St Leonard's, near Hastings, and sent in a letter to his sister Mary on 11 April 1860.*

*More important, for the way in which they led him to photography,
were visits he would pay to his maternal uncle, the bachelor lawyer,
Skeffington. He wrote to his sister Elizabeth about one such visit.*

### 4 ALFRED PLACE, LONDON
### 24 JUNE 1852

Dearest Elizabeth,

   . . .Uncle S came about ½ an hour after my arrival, looking very
well, and if anything, *rather* stouter than when I last saw him. He has
as usual got a great number of new oddities, including a lathe,
telescope stand, crest stamp (see the top of this notesheet), a
beautiful little pocket instrument for measuring distances on a map,
refrigerator, etc., etc. We had an observation of the moon and Jupiter
last night, and afterwards live animalcula in his large microscope: this
is a most interesting sight, as the creatures are most conveniently
transparent, and you see all kinds of organs jumping about like a
complicated piece of machinery, and even the circulation of
the blood. Everything goes on at railway speed, so I suppose
they must be some of those insects that only live a day or
two, and try to make the most of it . . .

Your most affectionate Brother,
Charles L. Dodgson

ABOVE: *Dodgson's photograph of his
Aunt Lucy, perhaps using Uncle
Skeffington's microscope. On the
death of Charles's mother (her sister)
in January 1851, this 'excellent
creature' had moved to Croft and
devoted herself to looking after
the family.*

*Dodgson's attempt to photograph Alice Liddell and her sisters in the
Deanery garden at the end of April 1856 was made with his friend
Southey's camera. His own arrived on 1 May and he soon began
to experiment with it, recording his progress in his diary.*

### DIARY 15 MAY (Th) 1856

Took several likenesses in the day, but all more or less failures.

### DIARY 3 JUNE (Tu) 1856

Spent the morning at the Deanery, photographing the children.

✦

*His camera soon led him to other children. While staying with his
Uncle Hassard in Putney, he met the Murdochs; the Lidells' governess
later introduced the Aclands.*

### DIARY 19 JUNE (Th) 1856

The Murdochs [Alice, aged 4, her sisters Katherine and Millicent and
her brother Charles] were brought over in the afternoon to be
photographed and stayed for the evening!

✦

### DIARY 3 NOV (M) 1856

Met Miss Prickett, the governess at the Deanery, walking with Ina,
and settled that I would come over on Wednesday morning if it is fine.
I also asked her to try and secure some of the Aclands coming over to
be taken: there are five or six of them, and Southey says they are a
beautiful family . . .

✦

*At Ripon during the Easter vacation of 1858 he befriended
yet more children.*

### DIARY 29 MAR (M) 1858

. . .called on the Maisters at Littlethorpe to ask the Miss Maisters to
bring over Kathleen Tidy tomorrow, as I want to secure getting at
least one good picture . . .

✦

*Kathleen Tidy, daughter of Major Thomas Tidy, became a child-
friend. Three years later he wrote to her for her tenth birthday.*

### CHRIST CHURCH, OXFORD
### 30 MARCH 1861

My dear Kathleen,

I promised once, if you remember, to send you one of these little
penknives on your next birthday, and I hope this will arrive in time. I
send with it my wishes for your good health, and many happy returns

RIGHT: *Cottages at Coniston in the
Lake District, painted by John Henry
Mole (1814–86). It was near
Coniston, at Tent Lodge, that
Dodgson introduced himself to
Tennyson in 1857, in the hope of
being allowed to photograph the great
man. He later pursued him to the
Isle of Wight.*

of your 72nd birthday. (Do not be surprised at my knowing your age: Henrietta told me, or I should never have guessed it) . . .

I will tell you a few ways in which you will find it useful. First, you should cut your meat at dinner with it: in this way you will be safe from eating too much, and so making yourself ill . . . Then you might be in danger of tiring yourself by walking too far — but now, by simply making a rule always *to cut your name on every tree you come to*, I am sure you will never go far enough to do yourself any harm . . .

Your affectionate friend,
Charles L. Dodgson

◆

*Dodgson's letter to his sister Mary records his pursuit of Tennyson.*

### AMBLESIDE
### 29 SEPTEMBER 1857

My dear Mary,

I am writing with the idea that this may reach you on Thursday morning. If it does not, I shall be home first, as I go on to Penrith this evening, and so home by Barnard Castle. Yesterday I took a portrait of Alfred Tennyson, which I think successful: also another of Hallam; and a group of the Marshalls, Mr Tennyson and Hallam; and others. I have got AT to write his name in my album, to go under his picture.

Your affectionate Brother,
Charles L. Dodgson

✦

*To his cousin, William E. Wilcox*

CHRIST CHURCH, OXFORD
11 MAY 1859

My dear William,

I have had it in my head for some time back to write you an account of my visit to the Isle of Wight . . . Wilfred must have basely misrepresented me if he said that I followed the Laureate down to his retreat, as I went, not knowing that he was there, to stay with an old College friend at Freshwater. Being there, I had the inalienable right of a freeborn Briton to make a morning call, which I did, in spite of my friend Collyns having assured me that the Tennysons had not yet arrived. There was a man painting the garden railing when I walked up to the house, of whom I asked if Mr Tennyson were at home, fully expecting the answer 'no,' so that it was an agreeable surprise when he said 'he's there, sir' and pointed him out, and behold! he was not many yards off, mowing his lawn in a wide-awake and spectacles. I had to introduce myself, as he is too short-sighted to recognise people . . . He took me over the house to see the pictures, etc. (among which my photographs of the family were hung 'on the line,' framed in those enamel — what do you call them — cartons?). The view from the garret windows he considers one of the finest in the island, and showed me a picture which his friend Richard Doyle had painted of it for him, also his little smoking-room at the top of the house, where of course he offered me a pipe, also the nursery, where we found the beautiful little Hallam (his son) who remembered me more readily than his father had done. . .

The next day I went to dinner, and met Sir John Simeon, who has an estate some miles off there, an old Christ Church man, who has turned Roman Catholic since. He is one of the pleasantest men I ever met, and you may imagine that the evening was a delightful one: I enjoyed it thoroughly, especially the concluding 2 hours in the smoking-room.

I took over my books of photographs, but Mrs Tennyson was too tired to look at them that evening, and I settled to leave them and come for them next morning, when I could see more of the children, who had only appeared for a few minutes during dinner.

Tennyson told us that often on going to bed after being engaged on composition, he had dreamed long passages of poetry ('you, I suppose,' turning to me, 'dream photographs') which he liked very much at the time, but forgot entirely when he woke. One was an enormously long one on fairies, where the lines from being very long at first, gradually got shorter and shorter, till it ended with 50 or 60 lines of 2 syllables each!

Up in the smoking-room the conversation turned upon murders, and Tennyson told us several horrible stories from his own experience: he seems rather to revel in such descriptions — one would not guess it from his poetry.

So no more at present from

Your faithful Cousin,
Charles L. Dodgson

*The 'Beggar-child' photograph about which Dodgson wrote to Mrs Tennyson was almost certainly the one taken of Alice Liddell as a beggar-child which survives.*

CHRIST CHURCH, OXFORD
4 JUNE 1859

Dear Mrs Tennyson,

I am thinking of sending a print of my photograph of Hallam (and possibly one of the group of him and Lionel) to be coloured by the

RIGHT: *Dodgson's famous photograph of Alice Liddell as a beggar-child, which Tennyson said was the most beautiful photograph he had ever known. This print has been tinted, as Dodgson mentioned in a letter to Mrs Tennyson, but by whom is not known.*

artist whose handiwork you saw a specimen of in the 'Beggar-child.' As I cannot trust my memory sufficiently to name the exact colour of their hair and eyes, would you kindly give me that information when you happen to have time to write? . . .

Very truly yours,
Charles L. Dodgson

LEFT: *The three Liddell sisters, Alice (left), Lorina (centre) and Edith (right), photographed by Dodgson as gypsy girls. Dodgson's diaries covering the period from April 1858 to May 1862 are missing, so we have no record of the most important period of his developing relationship with Alice Liddell. The acrostic (opposite page) suggests that the friendship had deepened steadily.*

◆

*In April 1862 Dodgson reported to his sister Mary on his second visit to the Tennyson home at Freshwater, Isle of Wight.*

### FRESHWATER, ISLE OF WIGHT
### 19 APRIL 1862

My dear Mary,

... *After* luncheon (not having been invited to that meal) I went to the Tennysons, and got Hallam and Lionel to sign their names in my album. Also I made a bargain with Lionel, that he was to give me some MS of his verses, and I was to send him some of mine. It was a very difficult bargain to make. I almost despaired of it at first, he put in so many conditions. 1st I was to play a game of chess with him — this with much difficulty was reduced to '12 moves on each side,' but this made little difference, as I check-mated him at the 6th move. 2nd he was to be allowed to give me one blow on the head with a mallet (this he at last consented to give up). I forget if there were others, but it ended in my getting the verses . . .

Your very affectionate brother,
Charles L. Dodgson

✦

*But throughout this period of his life it was the Liddell girls who remained Dodgson's favourite photographic models and child-friends. For Christmas 1861 he sent them* Holiday House, *by Catherine Sinclaire, with this acrostic inscribed on the inside cover.*

**L**ittle maidens, when you look
**O**n this little story-book,
**R**eading with attentive eye
**I**ts enticing history,
**N**ever think that hours of play
**A**re your only **HOLIDAY**
**A**nd that in a **HOUSE** of joy
**L**essons serve but to annoy:
**I**f in any **HOUSE** you find
**C**hildren of a gentle mind,
**E**ach the others pleasing ever —
**E**ach the others vexing never —
**D**aily work and pastime daily
**I**n their order taking gaily —
**T**hen be very sure that they
**H**ave a *Life* of **HOLIDAY**.

✦

# Alice in Wonderland

### JULY 1862–1868

LEFT: *English river scene in summer. It was up and down the Thames that Dodgson and his friends would take the Liddell girls on boating trips and tell them stories. One such story was about a little girl called Alice and the adventures she had on falling down a rabbit-hole.*

RIGHT: *'It was all very well to say "Drink Me," but the wise little Alice was not going to do that in a hurry. "No I'll look first," she said, "and see whether it's marked 'poison' or not."' Tenniel's illustration for* Alice's Adventures in Wonderland, *later coloured for* The Nursery 'Alice'.

All in the golden afternoon
  Full leisurely we glide;
For both our oars, with little skill,
  By little arms are plied,
While little hands make vain pretence
  Our wanderings to guide . . .
Thus grew the tale of Wonderland:
  Thus slowly, one by one,
Its quaint events were hammered out —
  And now the tale is done,
And home we steer, a merry crew,
  Beneath the setting sun.

THE FAMOUS RIVER EXPEDITION on the Thames, during the course of which Dodgson first told *Alice* stories to Alice Liddell and two of her sisters (Edith and Lorina), took place on 4 July 1862. Years later Dodgson wrote:

I distinctly remember . . . how, in a desperate attempt to strike out some new line of fairy-lore, I had sent my heroine straight down a rabbit-hole, to begin with, without the least idea what was to happen afterwards . . . Full many a year has slipped away, since that 'golden afternoon' that gave thee birth, but I can call it up almost as clearly as if it were yesterday — the cloudless blue above, the watery mirror below, the boat drifting idly on its way, the tinkle of the drops that fell from the oars, as they waved so sleepily to and fro, and (the one bright gleam of life in all the slumberous scene) the three eager faces, hungry for news of fairy-land . . .

Alice Liddell, by then Mrs Hargreaves, also remembered the occasion:

> I believe the beginning of *Alice* was told one summer afternoon when the sun was so burning that we had landed in the meadows down the river, deserting the boat to take refuge in the only bit of shade to be found, which was under a new-made hayrick. Here, from all three [sisters] came the old petition, 'Tell us a story,' and so began the ever-delightful tale. Sometimes to tease us — and perhaps being really tired — Mr Dodgson would stop suddenly and say, 'And that's all till next time.' 'Ah, but it is next time,' would be the exclamation from all three; and after some persuasion the story would start afresh. Another day, perhaps the story would begin in the boat, and Mr Dodgson, in the middle of telling a thrilling adventure would pretend to go fast asleep, to our great dismay.

It was not the first expedition Dodgson and the children had made that summer. About a fortnight before, they had gone downriver to Nuneham, accompanied by Dodgson's friend Duckworth, his sisters Fanny and Elizabeth and his aunt Lucy. In his diary for 17 June Dodgson wrote:

> We set out about 12.30 and got to Nuneham about 2: dined there, then walked in the park and set off for home about 4.30. About a mile above Nuneham heavy rain came on, and after bearing it a short time I settled that we had better leave the boat and walk: three miles of this drenched us all pretty well. I went on first with the children, as they could walk much faster than Elizabeth, and took them to the only house I knew in Sandford, Mrs Broughton's . . . I left them with her to get their clothes dried, and went off to find a vehicle . . . We all had tea in my rooms about 8.30.

Though this expedition predates the telling of *Alice*, the drenching of the party contributed to the story. Among the creatures nearly

ABOVE: *Robinson Duckworth, Fellow of Trinity College. He went on the famous river trip of 4 July 1862, when Dodgson began to tell the stories that became* Alice's Adventures in Wonderland. *He received a copy of the finished book inscribed, 'The Duck from the Dodo'.*

ABOVE: *Dodgson, a self-portrait taken c.1863, when he was thirty-one, at his father's rectory at Croft in Yorkshire.*

drowned in Alice's pool of tears are a Duck (Duckworth), a Do-do (Dodgson), a Lory (Lorina), and an Eaglet (Edith).

None of Dodgson's letters refer to the expedition of 4 July, but it is recorded in his diary:

> Duckworth and I made an expedition *up* the river to Godstow with the three Liddells: we had tea on the bank there, and did not reach Christ Church again till quarter past eight, when we took them on to my rooms to see my collection of micro-photographs, and restored them to the Deanery just before nine.

To this entry Dodgson later added:

> On which occasion I told them the fairy-tale of *Alice's Adventures Under Ground*, which I undertook to write out for Alice and which is now finished (as to the text) though the pictures are not yet nearly done.

Alice must have made her request that day because the following day, on the 9.02 train to London, he began to plan the book. But clearly a story as long and complex as *Alice's Adventures in Wonderland* could not

RIGHT: *Oxford boating party. 'It was high time to go, for the pool was getting quite crowded with the birds and animals that had fallen into it: there was a Duck and a Dodo, a Lory and an Eaglet, and several other curious creatures.'* Alice's Adventures in Wonderland

have been told even in outline on a single afternoon, and early in August he and the children made two more river expeditions, during which Alice's adventures were continued. Nor did he at once start to write them down; only on 13 November did he record:

> On returning to Christ Church I found Ina, Alice and Edith in the quadrangle, and had a little talk with them — a rare event of late. Began writing the fairy-tale for Alice, which I told them July 4, going to Godstow . . .

By February the following year he had completed a first draft of 18,000 words. It was this handwritten version that he eventually gave Alice on 26 November 1864, and called *Alice's Adventures Under Ground*. Meanwhile he had shown it to his friend, the poet and novelist George MacDonald. The MacDonalds were enthusiastic — their son Greville remembered saying he wished there were 60,000 volumes of it — and, by June, Dodgson had begun negotiating with the Clarendon Press about its printing. During the next twelve months he set about increasing it to its eventual 35,000 words. He also changed its title to *Alice's Adventures in Wonderland*. And early in 1864 he invited John Tenniel, *Punch*'s leading cartoonist, to illustrate it.

This did not stop him from preparing and adding to the manuscript of *Alice's Adventures Under Ground* thirty-seven illustrations of his own. The month after he had finished the text he 'called at the Deanery to arrange about our expedition tonight, and to borrow a Natural History to help in illustrating *Alice's Adventures* . . .'

Human beings, though, Dodgson was soon advised to draw from life. It might seem likely that he would have used Alice Liddell as a model, but she had short dark hair and was, anyway, ten — three years older than the Alice of the book. It is more probable, therefore, that Dodgson drew her younger sister, Edith, who had the well-known long fair hair of Tenniel's — and of his own — drawings.

In May 1864 Dodgson began to send Tenniel galley proofs of the book. Macmillan had agreed to publish it, but because Dodgson had undertaken to pay the artist it was he who instructed Tenniel, giving

ABOVE: '*It was the white rabbit coming back again, splendidly dressed, with a pair of white kid gloves in one hand and a nosegay in the other.*' Dodgson's own illustration from the original manuscript version of Alice, Alice's Adventures Under Ground.

ABOVE: *Calendar of events connected with the composing and publishing of* Alice's Adventures in Wonderland.

him continual directions and even sending him a photograph of a girl — Mary Hilton Badcock — who would make a suitable model. Tenniel used no model and it was Dodgson's guidance which ensured that his Alice resembled Dodgson's conception of her.

He had hoped to have to have the book published by the Christmas of that year, but Tenniel only produced the final illustrations in mid-June 1865. The Clarendon Press then worked fast, and before the end of the month had printed 2,000 copies. Just three years after he had first told *Alice* stories to the Liddell girls he was able to present Alice with a copy bound in white vellum.

That by no means ended the saga of the first edition of *Alice's Adventures in Wonderland*. Within a month Tenniel had reported that he was 'entirely dissatisfied with the printing of the pictures'. After much discussion, Dodgson ordered a new edition and agreed to the first edition being offered to an American publisher. The new edition was ready for Christmas 1865. Alice Liddell's copy of the first edition was removed from its vellum binding so that a second edition could be substituted. By the end of 1866 the new edition had sold 5,000 copies and Dodgson had recovered the heavy cost which he himself had borne of having it printed by a new printer.

On the surface all seemed to have turned out well, but the progress and final success of *Alice's Adventures in Wonderland* coincided with a crisis in Dodgson's relations with Alice Liddell. In late June 1863, less than a year after the famous boat trip, he, the children and various friends made another boat trip to Nuneham. His diary records:

> About 10 o'clock Alice and Edith came over to my rooms to fetch me over to arrange about an expedition to Nuneham. It ended in our going down at 3, a party of ten. We had our tea under the trees at Nuneham, after which the rest drove home in the carriage ... while Ina, Alice, Edith and I (*mirabile dictu*!) walked down to Abingdon-road station, and so home by railway: a pleasant expedition, with a *very* pleasant conclusion.

ABOVE: '"Come! there's no use in crying!" said Alice to herself rather sharply, "I advise you to leave off this minute!" (she generally gave herself very good advice, and sometimes scolded herself so severely as to bring tears into her eyes ...)' Alice's Adventures Under Ground

ABOVE: 'She did not get hold of anything, but she heard a little shriek and a fall and a crash of breaking glass, from which she concluded that it was just possible it had fallen into a cucumber-frame, or something of the sort.' Alice's Adventures Under Ground

The following day Dodgson asked their mother to send them over to be photographed. Her answer is not known because a page in his journal has been cut out and the previous page made to conclude, in handwriting which is not his own, to suggest that nothing is missing. It seems a fair guess that Mrs Liddell had become concerned about the nature of Dodgson's friendship with Alice, and had imposed limits on it. The Liddells then went to Llandudno for the long vacation and Dodgson does not mention them for almost six months. Then he reported on 5 December:

> Christ Church theatricals ... Mrs Liddell and the children were there — but I held aloof from them as I have done all this term.

And a fortnight later:

> At five went over to the Deanery, where I stayed till eight, making a sort of dinner at their tea. The nominal object of my going was to play croquet, but it never came to that ... Mrs Liddell was with us part of the time. It is nearly six months (June 25th) since I have seen anything of them, to speak of. I mark this day with a white stone.

◆

*It was to Tom Taylor, a well-known comic playwright of the time, that Dodgson wrote when he decided that he must look for a professional artist for the publication of the expanded* Alice *story.*

CHRIST CHURCH, OXFORD
20 DECEMBER 1863

Dear Sir,

Do you know Mr Tenniel enough to be able to say whether he could undertake such a thing as drawing a dozen wood-cuts to illustrate a child's book, and if so, could you put me into communication with him? ... I have written such a tale for a young friend, and illustrated it in pen and ink. It has been read and liked by so many children, and I have been so often asked to publish it, that I have decided on doing so. I have tried my hand at drawing on the wood, and come to the conclusion that it would take much more time than I can afford, and that the result would not be satisfactory after all. I want some figure-pictures done in pure outline, or nearly so, and of all artists on wood, I should prefer Mr Tenniel. If he should be willing to undertake them, I would send him the book to look over, not that he should at all follow my pictures, but simply to give him an idea of the sort of thing I want . . .

Very truly yours,
C. L. Dodgson

ABOVE: "'You are old, father William," the young man said,|"And your hair is exceedingly white:|And yet you incessantly stand on your head—|Do you think, at your age, it is right?"' Dodgson's own illustration, from Alice's Adventures Under Ground.

---

### DIARY 25 JAN 1864

Called at the 'Board of Health' and saw Mr Tom Taylor. He gave me a note of introduction to Mr Tenniel . . .

---

### DIARY 5 APRIL 1864

Heard from Tenniel that he consents to draw the pictures for *Alice's Adventures Under Ground* . . .

---

*Whatever injunction Mrs Liddell had put on his relations with her daughter in 1863, Dodgson now hoped that it no longer applied. Duckworth had accompanied Dodgson and the Liddell girls on the famous boating trip of 4 July 1862.*

### CHRIST CHURCH, OXFORD
### 12 APRIL 1864

Dear Duckworth,

Will you dine with me in Hall on Thursday? or on Saturday? And should you be disposed any day soon for a row on the river, for which I could procure some Liddells as companions.

Ever truly yours,
C. L. Dodgson

ABOVE: *Dodgson's photograph of Tom Taylor, the playwright and friend who gave him an introduction to the illustrator of the* Alice *books, John Tenniel.*

RIGHT: *Mary Macdonald, supposedly dreaming of her father George and brother Ronald, as photographed by Dodgson.*

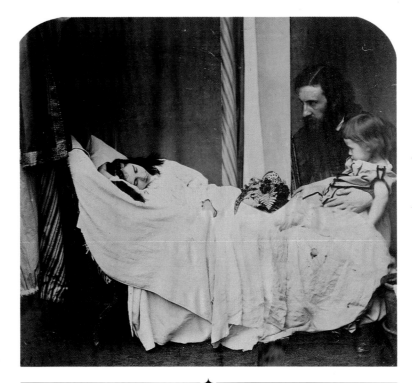

RIGHT: *Dodgson's photograph of himself with members of the MacDonald family (Mrs George MacDonald, wife of the poet and novelist, with, from left to right, her children Greville, Mary, Irene and Grace), taken at the MacDonalds' Hampstead home in 1863. The whole family shared Dodgson's sense of the ridiculous and became his close friends; the children even called him 'Uncle Dodgson'. It was the MacDonalds who first read the early draft of* Alice's Adventures in Wonderland *and encouraged Dodgson to publish it.*

### DIARY 12 MAY 1864

During these last few days I have applied in vain for leave to take the children on the river, i.e. Alice, Edith and Rhoda [the Liddell's fourth daughter]: but Mrs Liddell will not let *any* come in future — rather superfluous caution.

*Mary MacDonald was the second daughter of George MacDonald, who had first encouraged Dodgson to expand and publish* Alice's Adventures Under Ground. *There were eleven MacDonald*

*children, and Dodgson became an unofficial uncle to all of them, though Mary was his favourite. Aged eleven at the time of receiving the following letters, she died of tuberculosis at the age of twenty-four.*

CHRIST CHURCH, OXFORD
23 MAY 1864

My dear Child,

It's been so frightfully hot here that I've been almost too weak to hold a pen, and even if I had been able, there was no ink — it had all evaporated into a cloud of black steam, and in that state it has been floating about the room, inking the walls and ceiling till they're hardly fit to be seen: today it is cooler, and a little has come back into the ink-bottle in the form of black snow — there will soon be enough for me to write and order those photographs your Mamma wants.

This hot weather makes me very sad and sulky: I can hardly keep my temper sometimes. For instance, just now the Bishop of Oxford came in to see me — it was a civil thing to do, and he meant no harm, poor man: but I was so provoked at his coming in that I threw a book at his head, which I am afraid hurt him a good deal (Mem: this isn't quite true, so you needn't believe it. Don't be in such a hurry to believe next time — I'll tell you why. If you set to work to believe everything, you will tire out the believing-muscles of your mind, and then you'll be so weak you won't be able to believe the simplest true things. Only last week a friend of mine set to work to believe Jack-the-giant-killer. He managed to do it, but he was so exhausted by it that when I told him it was raining (which was true) he *couldn't* believe it, but rushed out into the street without his hat or umbrella, the consequence of which was his hair got seriously damp, and one curl didn't recover its right shape for nearly 2 days. (Mem: some of *that* is not quite true, I'm afraid.) . . .

With my kind regards to your Papa and Mamma, and love to you and the other infants, I remain

Your affectionate friend,
Charles L. Dodgson

ABOVE: *Greville MacDonald, son of George, as photographed by Dodgson. On first hearing* Alice *read to him by his mother, he said that 'he wished there were 60,000 volumes of it.'*

ABOVE: *Dodgson's portrait of Irene MacDonald. He once told her brother Greville (the model for Alexander Munro's 'Boy with the Dolphin' statue in Hyde Park) that if he too had a marble head, he need never comb his hair again.*

*To Mary MacDonald*
CHRIST CHURCH, OXFORD
14 NOVEMBER 1864

My dear Mary,

Once upon a time there was a little girl, and she had a cross old Uncle — his neighbours called him a Curmudgeon (whatever that may mean) — and this little girl had promised to copy out for him a sonnet Mr Rossetti had written about Shakespeare. Well, and she didn't do it, you know: and the poor old Uncle's nose kept getting longer and longer, and his temper getting shorter and shorter, and post after post went by, and no sonnet came — I leave off here to explain how they sent letters in those days: there were no gates, so the gate-posts weren't obliged to stay in one place — consequence of which, they went wandering all over the country — consequence of which, if you wanted to send a letter anywhere, all you had to do was to fasten it on to a gate-post that was going in the proper direction ... This was called 'sending a letter by the post.' They did things very simply in those days: if you had a lot of money, you just dug a hole under the hedge, and popped it in: then you said you had 'put it in the bank,' and you felt quite comfortable about it. And the way they travelled was — there were railings all along the side of the road, and they used to get up, and walk along the top, as steadily as they could, till they tumbled off — which they mostly did very soon. This was called 'travelling by rail.' Now to return to the wicked little girl. The end of her was, that a great black WOLF came, and — I don't like to go on, but nothing was found of her afterwards, except 3 small bones.

I make no remark. It is rather a horrid story.

Your loving friend,
C. L. Dodgson

ABOVE: *Dodgson's photograph of George MacDonald at work. He first met MacDonald in 1859 on a visit to a speech correctionist.*

LEFT AND FAR LEFT: *This grotesque old woman (far left), painted c.1500 by Quentin Massys, was evidently the model for Tenniel's Duchess (left). Massys's sitter is believed to have been Margaretha 'Maultasch', or 'pocket-mouth', popularly recorded as the ugliest woman in history. As for the Cheshire Cat (sitting by the Duchess), Dodgson may have been inspired by John Catheral of Chester, a man famous for his grin, after whom Cheshire cheeses used to be made in the shape of a grinning cat.*

*'Snowdrop' may have been Mary MacDonald's kitten and the original of Alice's kitten in the first chapter of* Through the Looking-Glass, *or it may have been the title of a play which Mary's mother had written for her children to perform.*

CHRIST CHURCH, OXFORD
22 JANUARY 1866

My dear Mary,

I am very glad you like the new copy of *Alice's Adventures*, and I should like very much to come and see you all again, and 'Snowdrop', if I could find the time, which I can't at present. But, by the bye, it's your turn to come and see *me* now . . .

Now I want to know what you *mean* by calling yourself 'naughty' for not having written sooner! Naughty, indeed! Stuff and nonsense! Do you think *I'd* call myself naughty, if I hadn't written to you, say for 50 years? Not a bit! I'd just begin as usual 'My dear Mary. 50 years ago you asked me what to do for your kitten, as it had a tooth-ache, and I have just remembered to write about it. Perhaps the tooth-ache has gone off by this time — if not, wash it carefully in hasty-pudding, and give it 4 pin-cushions boiled in sealing-wax, and just dip the end of its tail in hot coffee. This remedy has never been known to fail. There! *That's* the proper way to write! . . .

With kindest regards to your Papa and Mamma, and best love to your brothers and sisters, I remain

Your loving friend,
Charles L. Dodgson

ABOVE: *Mary Hilton Badcock, photographed by Dodgson. He told Tenniel that he thought she would make a good model for his drawings of Alice. Tenniel ignored this and many other of Dodgson's suggestions.*

*Meanwhile, in June 1864, Dodgson had asked Tom Taylor for more help — in finding him both subjects to photograph and a title for his book.*

CHRIST CHURCH, OXFORD
10 JUNE 1864

My dear Sir,

You were kind enough to wish me to let you know some while before I came to town on my photographic visit, that you might see whether you could entrap any victims for me. My plans are not definitely settled yet, but, so far as I can see, I shall be in town on or before the 20th (though I could come sooner if there were reason to do so). After that I shall be photographing at various friends' houses for 2 or 3 weeks . . .

Ever truly yours,
C. L. Dodgson

P.S. I should be very glad if you could help me in fixing on a name for my fairy-tale, which Mr Tenniel (in consequence of your kind introduction) is now illustrating for me, and which I hope to get published before Xmas. The heroine spends an hour underground, and meets various birds, beasts, etc. (*no* fairies), endowed with speech. The whole thing is a dream, but *that* I don't want revealed till the end. I first thought of 'Alice's Adventures Under Ground,' but that was pronounced too like a lesson-book, in which instruction about mines would be administered in the form of a grill; then I took 'Alice's Golden Hour,' but that I gave up, having a dark suspicion that there is already a book called 'Lily's Golden Hours.' Here are the other names I have thought of:

Alice among the { elves / goblins }  Alice's { hour / doings / adventures }  in { elf-land / wonderland. }

Of all these I at present prefer 'Alice's Adventures in Wonderland.' In spite of your 'morality,' I want something sensational. Perhaps you can suggest a better name than any of these.

RIGHT: *Dante Gabriel Rossetti and family (from left to right, Dante Gabriel himself, his sister, Christina, mother, and brother, William Michael), photographed by Dodgson, who also befriended other leading members of the Pre-Raphaelite movement. Rossetti's house and garden in Chelsea swarmed with pet animals, and it may well have been his sleepy wombat which was the original of the Dormouse at the Hatter's tea party.*

◆

*By 1864 he had come to know Dante Gabriel Rossetti, the leading Pre-Raphaelite painter, and had photographed the Rossettis, along with many of their friends, examples of Rossetti's work, and even some of his models, at their Chelsea home. Here they kept all manner of animals including a wombat, which 'slept all day long in the epergne [central ornament] of the dining-room table', and which was probably the model for Dodgson's Dormouse.*

CROFT RECTORY, DARLINGTON
8 SEPTEMBER 1864

My dear Rossetti,

. . . Today I am sending you most of the photographs you ordered. I have yet to send you

2 of yourself
2 Mrs and Miss Rossetti
2 'head on pillow.'

For those sent, you will owe me £2. 3. 6. You can pay by P.O. order on Darlington, or you can leave it till I call again, as you prefer . . .

Sincerely yours,
C. L. Dodgson

RIGHT: *Sand dunes at Bonchurch, Isle of Wight. Dodgson sometimes spent his summer holidays on the Isle of Wight between 1862 and 1876. Initially, he was drawn to Tennyson and his family, who lived at Freshwater, but soon found that he made lots of new, young, friends as well, on the beach at Sandown.*

---

*In July 1864 Dodgson returned to Freshwater, Isle of Wight.*

### DIARY 27 JULY (W) 1864

Called at Farringford, but found only Mrs Tennyson who was very busy letter-writing . . .

---

*In August he wrote to his fifth sister, Louisa.*

### PLUMBLY'S HOTEL, FRESHWATER, ISLE OF WIGHT
### 3 AUGUST 1864

My dear Louisa,

. . . Every morning four little children go by from the fort down to the beach: they go by in a state of great excitement, brandishing wooden spades, and making savage noises: from that moment they disappear entirely . . . The only theory I can form is, that they all tumble into a hole somewhere, and continue excavating therein during the day: however that may be, I have once or twice come across them returning at night, in exactly the same state of excitement, and seemingly in quite as great a hurry to get home as they were before to get out. The evening noises they make sound to me very much like the morning noises, but I suppose they are different to them, and contain an account of the day's achievements . . .

Your very affectionate brother,
C. L. Dodgson

---

*The publishing of* Alice's Adventures in Wonderland *made slow progress, and involved much correspondence with his publisher, Alexander Macmillan.*

CHRIST CHURCH, OXFORD
11 NOVEMBER 1864

Dear Sir,

I have been considering the question of the *colour* of *Alice's Adventures*, and have come to the conclusion that *bright red* will be the best — not the best, perhaps, artistically, but the most attractive to childish eyes. Can this colour be managed with the same smooth, bright cloth that you have in green?

Truly yours,
C. L. Dodgson

*To Alexander Macmillan*

CHRIST CHURCH, OXFORD
20 NOVEMBER 1864

Dear Sir,

I fear my little book *Alice's Adventures in Wonderland* cannot appear this year. Mr Tenniel writes that he is hopeless of completing the pictures by Xmas. The cause I do not know, but he writes in great trouble, having just lost his mother, and I have begged him to put the thing aside for the present. Under these circumstances what time should you advise our aiming at for bringing out the book? Would Easter be a good time, or would it be better to get it out before then?

I liked the specimen of red cloth you sent. I have not yet seen *The Children's Garland*, but will look at it. Believe me

Yours truly,
C. L. Dodgson

ABOVE: *Alexander Macmillan, Dodgson's publisher, photographed c.1865, the year in which he first published* Alice's Adventures in Wonderland.

RIGHT AND FAR RIGHT: *'Drink Me' from the 1865 edition of* Alice *(right), which Tenniel persuaded Dodgson to withdraw because it was so poorly printed. The quality of the reprinted edition (far right) is much finer.*

*Georgina Balfour was twelve or thirteen when Dodgson wrote to her in 1865 to try to recover one of the forty-eight presentation copies of the first edition of* Alice's Adventures in Wonderland *he had sent out to friends earlier in the year. Her father was headmaster of a school at Houghton-le-Spring, County Durham.*

CHRIST CHURCH, OXFORD
14 NOVEMBER 1865

My dear Georgie,

Not long ago I wrote to ask you to accept a copy of *Alice's Adventures in Wonderland. Now* I write to ask you to send it back again. Queer, isn't it? but I am not mad, as perhaps you are thinking.

The fact is, the book was so badly printed, or rather the pictures, that I have had it all done again, and the new ones are *far* better than the old. So if you will send the old one back, you shall have a beautiful new one instead. Give my kind regards to your Mamma, and love to Ella.

Very truly yours,
C. L. Dodgson

*By mid-November the reprinted edition of* Alice's Adventures in Wonderland *was ready, and Dodgson was writing to Alexander Macmillan for reports of its reception. The novelist Henry Kingsley, who received one of the fifty presentation copies, said of the book, 'it is like gathering cowslips in springtime.'*

CHRIST CHURCH, OXFORD
19 NOVEMBER 1865

Dear Mr Macmillan,

The 50 copies, and the one bound in vellum, have all arrived safe. One of them is deficient of 16 pages (161 to 176). Who ought to be the loser by a mistake of that kind?

In case any papers or magazines should notice the book, I should wish to have copies to keep of the numbers containing the notices. Can you find any one to undertake to look out for them and collect them.

I shall be very much interested to hear whether you think the sale has made a good start or not. Believe me

Truly yours,
C. L. Dodgson

THE FIRST REVIEW of *Alice's Adventures in Wonderland* had appeared the previous day (18 November 1865). Others followed. *The Athenaeum*, 16 December 1865, concluded, 'We fancy that any real child might be more puzzled than enchanted by this stiff, over-wrought story.' A week later, however, *The Spectator* wrote that 'big folks who take it home to their little folks will find themselves reading more than they intended, and laughing more than they had any right to expect.' And the following 25 May *The Sunderland Herald* ran an even more favourable review:

This pretty and funny book ought to become a great favourite with children. It has this advantage, that it has no moral, and that it does not teach anything. It is, in fact, pure sugar throughout, and is without any of that bitter foundation which some people imagine ought to be at the bottom of all children's books.

ABOVE: *Dodgson used many sources to help him when he was illustrating the manuscript version of* Alice — *he must have seen this painting of a dodo hanging in Oxford's University Museum; he also borrowed a book of natural history from Dean Liddell.*

RIGHT: *Tenniel's drawing of the Dodo in* Alice's Adventures in Wonderland, *as subsequently coloured for* The Nursery 'Alice', *1890.*

*To Alexander Macmillan*

### CROFT RECTORY, DARLINGTON
### 24 AUGUST 1866

My dear Sir,

Thanks for your letter and information, with which I am very well satisfied. Your magnificent idea of printing *3000* more alarms me a little: *I* should have thought *1000* a large enough venture, considering the sale hitherto . . .

It will probably be some time before I again indulge in paper and print. I have, however, a floating idea of writing a sort of sequel to *Alice*, and if it ever comes to anything, I intend to consult you at the very outset, so as to have the thing properly managed from the beginning.

Sincerely yours,
C. L. Dodgson

Instance of hieroglyphic writing
of the date MDCCCLXVII
Interpretation. "There is a coat here,
left in the care of a Russian peasant,
which I should be glad to receive
from him"

*The following year, in 1867, Dodgson, with his friend HenryLiddon, made his only foreign tour — to Russia. On 6 August they arrived at Nijni Novgorod, to visit the famous fair, after a rail journey during which a broken bridge had forced them to walk a mile through soaking rain. He recorded the trip in his diary.*

### DIARY 6 AUG 1867

We went to the Smernovaya (or some such name) Hotel, a truly villainous place, though no doubt the best in the town. The feeding was very good, and everything else very bad. It was some consolation to find that as we sat at dinner we furnished a subject of the liveliest interest to six or seven waiters, all dressed in white tunics, belted at the waist, and white trousers, who ranged themselves in a row and gazed in a quite absorbed way at the collection of strange animals that were feeding before them. Now and then a twinge of conscience would seize them that they were, after all, not fulfilling the great object of life as waiters, and on these occasions they would all hurry to the end of the room, and refer to a great drawer which seemed to contain nothing but spoons and corks. When we asked for anything, they first looked at each other in an alarmed way; then, when they had ascertained which understood the order best, they all followed his example, which always was to refer to the big drawer . . .

But all the novelties of the day were thrown into the shade by our adventure at sunset, when we came upon the Tartar mosque (the only one in Nijni) exactly as one of the officials came out on the roof to utter the muezzin cry, or call to prayers. Even if it had been in no way singular in itself, it would have been deeply interesting from its novelty and uniqueness, but the cry itself was quite unlike anything I have ever heard before. The beginning of each sentence was uttered in a rapid monotone and towards the end it rose gradually till it ended in a prolonged, shrill wail, which floated overhead through the still air with an indescribably sad and ghostlike effect; heard at night, it would have thrilled one like the cry of the Banshee.

◆

*The number of Dodgson's child-friends continued to increase. Annie Rogers was ten or eleven when Dodgson forgot an appointment with her in 1867.*

My dear Annie,

. . . Why wasn't I there? Well the fact was this — I went out for a walk with Bibkins . . . A thought crossed my mind, and I said solemnly, 'Dobkins, what o'clock is it?' 'Three,' said Fipkins, surprised at my manner. Tears ran down my cheeks. 'It is the HOUR,' I said. 'Tell me, tell me, Hopkins, what day is it?' 'Why, Monday, of course,' said Lupkins. 'Then it is the DAY!' I groaned. I wept. I screamed . . . It was all over: I was brought home, in a cart, attended by the faithful Wopkins, in several pieces.

Your miserable friend,
Lewis Carroll

'Dolly' was Agnes Argles, fourth daughter of Marsham Argles, Rector of Barnack and Dean of Peterborough. Now aged nine or ten, she had asked Dodgson when he was going to write another book. The copy of Aunt Judy's Magazine *which he ordered for her contained 'Bruno's Revenge, the story which he eventually expanded into his two* Sylvie and Bruno *books.*

### CHRIST CHURCH, OXFORD
### 28 NOVEMBER 1867

Dear Miss Dolly,

I have a message for you from a friend of mine, Mr Lewis Carroll, who is a queer sort of creature, rather too fond of talking nonsense. He told me you had once asked him to write another book like one you had read — I forget the name — I think it was about 'malice.' 'Tell her,' he said, 'that I have just written a little story which is printed in *Aunt Judy's Magazine* and that I have ordered a copy to be sent to her.'

Yours very truly,
Charles L. Dodgson

ABOVE: *Dodgson's portrait of Dymphna Ellis, daughter of the Vicar of Cranbourne, taken c.1865. He thought 'Dymphna' an 'extraordinary name', and felt her first name (actually Frances) must be equally extravagant: 'What is "F" before "Dymphna"? Is it Fatima, Fenella or Feodora?'*

*Dodgson wrote this and other fairy-letters in miniature, on a sheet measuring 38 × 41mm. Dymphna Ellis was the daughter of the Vicar of Cranbourne, one of Dodgson's fellow photographers.*

### 2 DECEMBER 1867

Dear Miss Dymphna,

As Mr Dodgson has asked me to write for him, I send these few lines to say that he has sent you a copy of *Aunt Judy's Magazine,* that you may read the little story he has written about Bruno and me. Dear Miss Dymphna, if you will come down into our wood, I shall be very glad to see you, and I will show you the beautiful garden Bruno made for me.

Your affectionate little fairy-friend,
Sylvie

ABOVE: *One of the letters in fairy writing that Dodgson wrote to some of his young friends in the guise of 'Sylvie' from his Sylvie and Bruno stories. This one, dated 2 December 1867, to Dymphna Ellis, is reproduced slightly larger than actual size—it had to be read with a magnifying-glass.*

*The train Dodgson was catching had left Peterborough to take him back to London after his first visit to Dolly Argles and her family.*

### CHRIST CHURCH, OXFORD
#### 17 APRIL 1868

My dear Dolly,

You can't think how useful that present of yours was, all the way up to London! Perhaps you remarked that old lady who was sitting next me in the carriage? I mean the one with hooked eyes and a dark blue nose. Well, the moment the train went off, she said to me (by the by, it was her language that first made me think she wasn't *quite* a lady) she said to me, 'Was them three young ladies on the plank-form, what held their hankerchers to their eyes, a shedding crystal tears, or was they shamming?' I didn't like to correct her, even by speaking correctly myself, so I said, 'They *was* shedding real tears, mum, but tears ain't crystals.' She said, 'Young man, you hurts my feelings!' and she began crying.

I tried to comfort her by saying cheerfully, 'Now don't *you* shed crystal tears. Won't a little brandy do you good?' 'No!' she said. 'No

75

LEFT: *The Chestnuts, Guildford, to which Dodgson moved his family in 1868 after the death of his father. 'The greatest blow that has ever fallen on my life was the death ... of my own dear father,' he recalled.*

brandy — poetry, poetry!' So I got your book out, and handed it to her, and she read it all the rest of the way, only sobbing a little now and then . . .

Some children have a most disagreeable way of getting grown-up: I hope you won't do anything of that sort before we meet again . . .

Yours affectionately
C. L. Dodgson

♦

*To Edith Argles, Dolly's elder sister.*

### CROFT RECTORY, DARLINGTON
#### 24 JUNE 1868

My dear Edith,

I fear you (and specially Dolly, who wrote some time ago) will have thought me a careless correspondent, but Dolly's letter came when I was very busy, and so did yours too.

I am in great sorrow just now, as my dear dear father has been taken away from us. I am afraid I shall not be able to come to you this summer at Babbacombe, as it is too far south for my sisters to go too.

Give my love to Dolly, and kindest regards to your party.

Your sincere friend,
C. L. Dodgson

◆

*Dodgson's father died in June 1868. By December that year he had arranged and completed the family's move to Guildford, where he now invited Dolly Argles to pay a visit.*

### CHRIST CHURCH, OXFORD
### 11 DECEMBER 1868

My dear Dolly,

... In a week's time I am going down to 'The Chestnuts,' Guildford, where my sisters live, and I shall be there, or in London, till about January 20. Where shall you be all that time? Couldn't you persuade your inexorable father (you may look out that word in the dictionary, if you like) to bring Edith and you up to town? and we could easily coax you on then as far as Guildford — it *is* such a pretty place!

Well, as to the new volume of *Alice*, I am just going to begin printing it — and I *hope* Mr Tenniel will manage to get the pictures done by Christmas next year ...

Your loving friend,
C. L. Dodgson

◆

# Through the Looking-Glass

JUNE 1868–1872

LEFT: *Guildford in 1849. The town had changed little by 1868 when Dodgson moved his family there after the death of his father. As the oldest son, Dodgson was now the head of the family; and he continued to run The Chestnuts as the Dodgson family home for the rest of his life, though his work still tied him to Oxford.*

IN THE SAME MONTH THAT his father died (June 1868), Dodgson began the writing in full of *Behind the Looking-Glass, and What Alice Saw There*, as he at first called it. The idea for a second *Alice* book had been in his mind for some time; indeed, according to Alice Liddell, many of its stories had been invented before those of *Alice's Adventures in Wonderland*, and dated from 'the period when we were excitedly learning chess.' And a game of chess (or a chess lesson) forms the structure of the book.

As for the looking-glass theme, fifty years later his cousin, Alice Raikes, claimed that he thought of it one time when he met her in his Uncle Skeffington's house in Onslow Square; he told her to hold an orange in her right hand and then asked her in which hand the little girl in the mirror was holding it.

Later, she claimed that Dodgson himself had said this episode had given him the idea for *Through the Looking-Glass*. However, the most likely date of that meeting is 1871, and already, in May 1868, he had written in his diary that Sir Noël Paton was too ill to 'undertake the pictures for *Looking-glass House*'. If her claim is correct they must have had an earlier meeting.

Whatever the truth, it was in June 1868, when Tenniel agreed again to be the illustrator, that Dodgson began the proper writing of the book. A year and a half later, in January 1870, he sent Macmillan the first chapter of *Through the Looking-Glass*. After working on it through 1870 and half of 1871, he finally delivered the complete manuscript in June that year. The first printed copy reached him on 6 December, and two days later he received the presentation copies, including three in Morocco — one for Alice Liddell, one for Tennyson and the third for Florence Terry, the youngest sister of the actress, Ellen Terry.

ABOVE: *Tenniel's illustration of the Red King and Queen for* Through the Looking-Glass. *Dodgson had told Alice and her sisters stories based on chess characters even before the famous Thames boating expedition of July 1862 on which he began to tell them* Alice's Adventures in Wonderland.

LEFT: *The three older Liddell daughters as young ladies (from left to right, Edith, Alice and Lorina). They were widely renowned for their beauty and accomplishments, and Alice even attracted the attention of royalty. She and Queen Victoria's fourth son, Prince Leopold, first Duke of Albany, fell in love while the Prince was an undergraduate at Christ Church, but could not marry because she was a commoner.*

On 4 May 1871 Alice Liddell turned nineteen. Although he had continued to see her and her sisters, photographing Alice as late as 1870, contact had been only occasional and he had now been writing essentially both for and about a girl who was only a memory. He was surely writing about his own situation when he made the fictional Alice leave behind the old and pathetic White Knight in his shining armour to cross the brook and become a queen.

Alice never became a queen but she almost became a princess. In 1872 Prince Leopold, Queen Victoria's fourth son, matriculated at Christ Church, and soon afterwards he and Alice fell in love. Dodgson also met the prince. In 1875 he took his photograph, and allowed him to choose a number of prints from his collection. Whether he chose one of Alice is not known, but Dodgson must have expected that he would, for the romance was public knowledge. There was, however, little real chance that it might lead to marriage, for the Queen would have been most unlikely to allow Leopold, who was fourth in succession to the throne, to marry a commoner.

When eventually, in 1880, Alice married Reginald Hargreaves, a rich Christ Church undergraduate who played cricket for Hampshire, the prince sent her a ruby and diamond brooch as a wedding present. He named one of his daughters Alice, and Alice Hargreaves named her second son Leopold. Both this son and her eldest were killed in the First World War, but a third son survived, and she herself lived until 1934.

Whatever the reason, there is no doubt that as the years passed Dodgson became increasingly hostile to Dean and Mrs Liddell; the Dean must have found him one of the most cantankerous members of the Christ Church common room. The issues on which Dodgson opposed Liddell now seem trivial, and more interesting is the time and effort that Dodgson must have spent on his opposition. This took the form of writing and publishing a number of pamphlets, either anonymously or signed with false initials. On the title page of one of these, opposing a proposed new belfry at Christ Church for the bells of the cathedral, a project which Liddell supported, there appeared a

ABOVE: *"Well this is grand,"* said Alice. *"I never expected I should be a Queen so soon—"'* Through the Looking-Glass. *In memory of Alice Liddell, Prince Leopold named his daughter 'Alice'; she sent this photograph of herself and her brother to Dodgson.*

featureless square with the caption 'East view of the New Belfrey, Christ Church, as seen from the meadow.'

At the same time, from 1872 onwards, *Through the Looking-Glass* was becoming a success greater even than *Alice's Adventures in Wonderland*, and Dodgson even signed some of his letters to little friends as 'Lewis Carroll'.

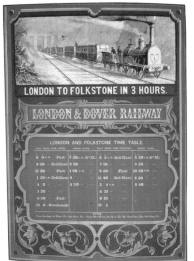

ABOVE: *Railways fascinated Dodgson, as they did most of his contemporaries. The first Stockton and Darlington train had run only seven years before he was born, and a railway game was one of the first amusements he invented for his brothers and sisters to play in the Rectory garden at Croft.*

RIGHT: *The bustle and confusion of William Powell Frith's 'The Railway Station' recalls his 'Derby Day', and suggests that for Victorians train travel was almost as exciting as a trip to the races.*

*Isabel Seymour was the daughter of a Fellow of All Souls'. She was about thirteen years old when Dodgson wrote to her in 1869. They had started their train journey from Oxford together, but parted at Reading, Dodgson to go to Guildford, Isabel to go on to Paddington, London.*

THE CHESTNUTS, GUILDFORD
15 MAY 1869

My dear Isabel,

Words cannot tell how horrified, terrified, petrified (everything ending with 'fied,' including all my sisters here saying 'fie!' when they heard of it) I was when I found that I had carried off your ticket to Guildford. I enquired directly I got there whether *anything* could be done, but found you must have arrived in London some time before I got here. So there was nothing to be done but tear my hair (there is almost none left now), weep, and surrender myself to the police.

I do *hope* you didn't suffer any inconvenience on account of my forgetfulness, but you see you *would* talk so all the way (though I begged you not) that you drove everything out of my head, including the very small portion of brain that is usually to be found there . . .

I hardly dare ask what really happened at Paddington, whether the gentleman and lady, who were in the carriage, helped you out of the difficulty, or whether your maid had money enough, or whether you had to go to prison. If so, never mind: I'll do my best to get you out, and at any rate you shan't be executed.

Seriously, I am *so* sorry for it, and with all sorts of apologies, I am

Sincerely yours,
C. L. Dodgson

*To Isabel Seymour*

CHRIST CHURCH, OXFORD
29 MAY 1869

My dear Isabel,

. . . I should like you to know the *real* reason of my having carried off your railway-ticket. You will guess by this, of course, that my last letter was all a hoax. Well, you told me, you know, that it was your *first* railway-journey alone: naturally that set me thinking, 'Now what can I do to give her a *really exciting adventure?*'

Now three plans occurred to me. The first was to wait till the train had started from Reading, and then fire a pistol through your carriage-window, so that the bullet might go near your head and startle you a little. But there were two objections to this plan — one, that I hadn't got a loaded pistol with me, the other, that the bullet *might* have gone in at a wrong window, and some people are so stupid, they might not have taken it as a joke.

The second plan was to give you, just as the train left Reading, what should look like a Banbury-cake, but should afterwards turn out to be a rattlesnake. The only objection to this plan was, that they didn't keep that kind at Reading . . .

The third plan was to keep the ticket, so that you might be alarmed when you got to London. Of course I arranged thoroughly with the Guard that the thing was not to be overdone. He was to look a little stern at first, and then gradually to let his expressive features kindle into a smile of benevolence. I was very particular on this point, and almost my last words to him were, 'Are you sure you can manage the benevolence?' and I made·him practise it several times on the platform before I would let him go.

Now you know my whole plan for making your journey a real *Adventure*. I only hope it succeeded . . .

Very truly yours,
C. L. Dodgson

P.S. I must tell you candidly that the whole of this letter is a hoax, and that my *real* reason was — to be able to make you a nice little portable present. Friends suggested a corkscrew, a work-box, or a harmonium: but, as I cleverly remarked, 'These are all very well in their way, but you can only use them *sometimes* — whereas a railway-ticket is *always* handy!' Have I chosen well?

◆

*Dodgson's relations with Tennyson continued to be ambivalent.*

CHRIST CHURCH, OXFORD
3 MARCH 1870

Dear Mr Tennyson,

... There is a certain unpublished poem of yours called 'The Window' which it seems was printed for private circulation only. However it has been transcribed, and is probably in many hands in the form of MS. A friend, who had had a MS copy given to him, has in his

*Interior of Railway carriage. (1st Class). Alice on seat by herself. Man in white paper. reading. & Goat very shadowy & indistinct — (with opera glass) sitting opposite. Beard looking in at windows.*

*My dear Dodgson.*
*I think that where the jump occurs in the*

turn presented me with one. I have not even read it yet, and shall do so with much greater pleasure when I know that you do not object to my possessing it. What I plead for is, first, that you will make me comfortable in possessing this copy by giving your consent to my preserving it — secondly, the further permission to *show* it to my friends. I can hardly go so far as ask for leave to give away copies of it to friends, though I should esteem such a permission as a great favour . . .

Very truly yours,
C. L. Dodgson

*In reply, Mrs Tennyson warned Dodgson against making 'a request which will only revive the annoyance he has already had on the subject and add to it.'*

RIGHT: '*My First Sermon*', *a famous painting of the period by the Pre-Raphaelite painter, Millais. In his drawing of Alice in the railway carriage (opposite), Tenniel has clearly parodied this picture; much of the detail is identical (the muff, the hat, its feather), but a pocket-book has been substituted for the Bible.*

*The man sitting opposite Alice, 'dressed in white paper', strongly resembles the Disraeli of Tenniel's* Punch *cartoons, who himself would have been surrounded by official 'white papers'.*

## CHRIST CHURCH, OXFORD
## 7 MARCH 1870

Dear Mr Tennyson,

... Understanding the letter I received this morning as coming really from yourself, though written by Mrs Tennyson, I must trouble you with one or two remarks on it.

First, let me express my sincere sympathy with you in all the annoyance that has been caused you by the unauthorised circulation of your unpublished poems. Whoever it was that thus wantonly betrayed the confidence you had reposed in him, he has, in my opinion, done a most dishonourable thing ...

I must in justice to myself call your attention to your concluding sentence. 'It would be well that, whatever may be done by such people, a gentleman should understand that, when an author does not give his works to the public, he has his own reasons for it.' This sentence certainly implies, however unintentionally, a belief that I have done something ungentlemanly. Let me then remind you that in all these matters I have been a purely passive agent, and that in all cases I have consulted your wishes and scrupulously followed them. It is by no act of mine that this poem is now in circulation, and that a copy of it has come into my hands. Under these circumstances I may fairly ask you to point out what I have failed to do that the most chivalrous sense of honour could require ...

With kind regards to Mrs Tennyson, I remain

Sincerely yours,
C. L. Dodgson

◆

*Tennyson's reply has not survived, but Dodgson's next letter proves that he had received one. On one side of the sheet he wrote a sort of dialogue.*

'Sir, you are no gentleman.'

'Sir, you do me grievous wrong by such words. Prove them, or retract them!'

ABOVE: *John Tenniel's self-portrait (1889). Best known today as the illustrator of the* Alice *books, in his day he was famous as* Punch's *leading cartoonist.*

RIGHT: *'As the Knight sang the last words of the ballad, he gathered up the reins, and turned his horse's head along the road by which they had come. "You've only a few yards to go," he said, "down the hill and over that little brook, and you'll be a Queen—But you'll stay and see me off first?" he added as Alice turned away with an eager look.' Tenniel's illustration of Alice saying 'goodbye' to the White Knight (clearly drawn as a caricature of the artist himself), from* Through the Looking-Glass. *The sadness of the scene suggests that Dodgson was writing of his own loss of the young Alice Liddell who had been his muse for so long.*

'I reiterate them. Your conduct has been dishonourable.'

'It is not so. I offer a full history of my conduct. I charge you with groundless libel: what say you to the charge?'

'I once believed even worse of you, but begin to think you may be a gentleman after all.'

'These new imputations are as unfounded as the former. Once more, what say you to the charge of groundless libel?'

'*I absolve you.* Say no more.'

*The other side is more formal.*

### 31 MARCH 1870

My dear Sir,

Thus it is, as it seems to me, that you first do a man an injury, and then forgive him — that you first tread on his toes, and beg him not to cry out!

Nevertheless I accept what you say, as being in substance, what it certainly is not in form, a retractation (though without a shadow of apology or expression of regret) of all dishonourable charges against me, and an admission that you had made them on unsufficient grounds.

Sincerely yours,
C. L. Dodgson

◆

*It was not until eighteen months later that Dodgson was able to tell Mrs Bradley (to whose daughter, Emily, Mrs Tennyson was godmother) that his quarrel with Tennyson was over.*

### CHRIST CHURCH, OXFORD
### 22 DECEMBER 1871

Dear Mrs Bradley,

My 'peace-offering' to Mr Tennyson was rewarded by a note of thanks from himself, and I am quite pleased with the result of my experiment. Have you given the Tennysons copies of my photographs of the children? If not, I should like to send Mrs Tennyson cartes of

ABOVE: *May Prinsep, later wife of the poet Alfred's eldest son, Hallam, painted walking on Afton Downs above Freshwater on the Isle of Wight by her cousin Valentine. Dodgson made two attempts to photograph Tennyson there, but the great poet was increasingly evasive.*

RIGHT: *Freshwater Bay from the east, a contemporary painting by John Carmichael.*

ABOVE: *Lionel Tennyson, photographed by Julia Margaret Cameron. Dodgson thought him 'the loveliest child, boy or girl, that I ever saw.'*

Emily and Hugh, which I think were the best. She would like to have one of her godchild . . .

Wishing you all a very happy Christmas, I am

Very truly yours,
C. L. Dodgson

---

*Six months later, he was offering Tennyson help with his son's stammer, suggesting a visit to Dr Lewin. Dodgson had attended one of Dr Lewin's lectures earlier that month at Nottingham. When Dodgson tested himself by reading aloud next day he was 'well pleased with the result.'*

CHRIST CHURCH, OXFORD
19 JUNE, 1872

Dear Mr Tennyson,

Though it is not much more than a week since I went to Dr Lewin and learnt his system for the cure of stammering, I am already quite convinced of its great value, and that almost any one, with resolution and perseverance, may be entirely cured by it. If Lionel is, as I understand, still suffering, as I have done for most of my life, from that most annoying malady, I do most strongly advise that he should go over to Sheffield and hear Dr Lewin. One lecture will in all probability be all that he will need, and he can then complete the cure for himself. Dr Lewin's charges vary with the circumstances of the patient: but he never asks *more* than £20.

The system is quite different from that of any other teacher that I have heard of, and is beautifully simple . . .

Very truly yours,
C. L. Dodgson

---

*Meanwhile Dodgson had continued to collect little girls for photographing, including Agnes and Amy Hughes, daughters of the artist Arthur Hughes. By 1871 Agnes, the younger of the two, was about nine and Amy about thirteen.*

ABOVE: *Hallam Tennyson, portrait by Dodgson.*

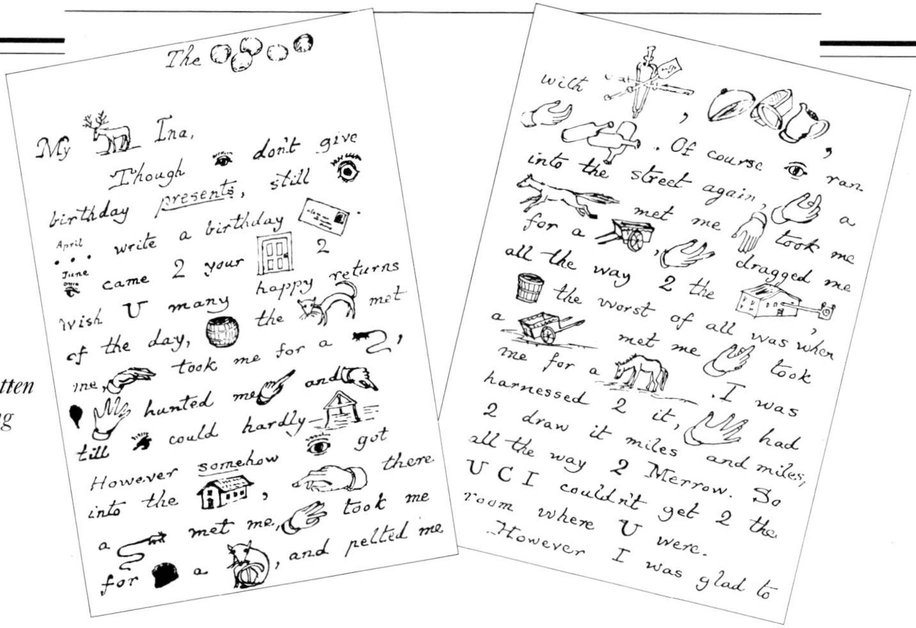

RIGHT: *Part of a rebus letter, written after 5 October 1869 to his young friend Georgina Watson.*

My dear Agnes,

. . . Three visitors came knocking at my door, begging me to let them in. And when I opened the door, who do you think they were? You'll never guess. Why, they were three cats! Wasn't it curious? However, they all looked so cross and disagreeable that I took up the first thing I could lay my hand on (which happened to be the rolling-pin) and knocked them all down as flat as pancakes! 'If *you* come knocking at *my* door,' I said, '*I* shall come knocking at *your* heads.' That was fair, wasn't it?

Yours affectionately,
Lewis Carroll

---

*To Agnes Hughes*

My dear Agnes,

About the cats, you know. Of course I didn't leave them lying flat on the ground like dried flowers: no, I picked them up, and I was as

kind as I could be to them. I lent them the portfolio for a bed — they wouldn't have been comfortable in a real bed, you know: they were too thin — but they were *quite* happy between the sheets of blotting-paper — and each of them had a pen-wiper for a pillow. Well, then I went to bed: but first I lent them the three dinner-bells, to ring if they wanted anything in the night . . .

In the morning I gave them some rat-tail jelly and buttered mice for breakfast, and they were as discontented as they could be. They wanted some boiled pelican, but of course I knew it wouldn't be good for them. So all I said was 'Go to Number Two, Finborough Road, and ask for Agnes Hughes, and if it's *really* good for you, she'll give you some.' Then I shook hands with them all, and wished them all goodbye, and drove them up the chimney. They seemed very sorry to go, and they took the bells and the portfolio with them. I didn't find this out till after they had gone, and then I was sorry too, and wished for them back again. What do I mean by 'them'? Never mind.

How are Arthur, and Amy, and Emily? Do they still go up and down Finborough Road, and teach the cats to be kind to mice? I'm *very* fond of all the cats in Finborough Road.

Give them my love.

Who do I mean by 'them'?

Never mind.

Your affectionate friend,
Lewis Carroll

LEFT, AND FAR RIGHT: "'*Let's pretend that you're the Red Queen, Kitty! Do you know, I think, if you sat up and folded your arms, you'd look exactly like her. Now do try, there's a dear!*'" Tenniel's *illustrations of Alice with Dinah the cat and her kittens Snowdrop and Kitty, for* Through the Looking-Glass. *The white kitten may well have been named after his young friend Mary MacDonald's kitten, Snowdrop.*

---

*Signing off a letter to Amy Hughes, Dodgson tried to entice his little friend into his own mathematical world.*

My dear Amy,

. . . You asked me after those three cats. Ah! The dear creatures! Do you know, ever since that night they first came, they have *never left me*? Isn't it kind of them? Tell Agnes this. She will be interested to hear it. And they *are* so kind and thoughful! Do you know, when I had gone out for a walk the other day, they got *all* my books out of the bookcase, and opened them on the floor, to be ready for me to read. They opened them all at page 50, because they thought that would be a nice useful page to begin at. It was rather unfortunate, though: because they took my bottle of gum, and tried to gum pictures upon the ceiling (which they thought would please me), and by accident they spilt a quantity of it all over the books. So when they were shut up and put by, the leaves all stuck together, and I can never read page 50 again in any of them!

However, they meant it very kindly, so I wasn't angry. I gave them each a spoonful of ink as a treat; but they were ungrateful for that, and made dreadful faces. But, of course, as it was given them as a treat, they had to drink it. One of them has turned black since: it was a white cat to begin with.

Give my love to any children you happen to meet. Also I send two kisses and a half, for you to divide with Agnes, Emily, and Godfrey. Mind you divide them fairly.

Yours affectionately,
C. L. Dodgson

♦

*In September 1871 he wrote to his sister Mary — because, as he put it, he used to consider her 'the proper recipient for any news of a specially artistic nature' — about a visit to the painter Sir Noël Paton, the artist he had once hoped would illustrate* Through the Looking-Glass. *The Patons and their eight children lived at Lamlash on the Isle of Arran.*

BRODICK HOTEL, ISLE OF ARRAN
19 SEPTEMBER, 1871

My dearest Mary,

... Both he and Lady Paton are thoroughly genuine and very charming. What I call 'real' people are rare, and I delight in them when found. He is a grand-looking man, tall and strong, looking much more of a soldier than an artist. His children are most complete 'children of nature.' They are quite unique in my experience — something like South Sea Islanders with the instincts of gentlemen

and ladies: no 'manners,' but simple natural politeness. I can't quite describe it, but it charmed me very much, as being thoroughly 'real.' The eldest girl, Mona, about II, would make a grand subject for a picture — rather a melancholy expression (as all Scotch children have), but the very picture of rude health. We all went out in a heavy sailing-boat, which had to be rowed mostly, there was so little wind, and she and I pulled it some way, and I had fairly hard work to pull equally with her. Many of Sir N. P.'s pictures contain the children. I had *such* a treat in Edinburgh, by his invitation, in visiting his studio there, and looking over a number of pencil drawings, some only half-finished, a kind which always interests me much more than finished pictures... When I left I was fairly good friends with all the children, as well as with their parents, and Mona asked in broad Scotch, 'When are ye comin' again?'...

Your loving brother,
C. L. Dodgson

ABOVE AND BELOW: *Tenniel's original sketch in pencil on tracing paper of the Red King asleep in* Through the Looking-Glass *(above), and the final version as transferred to the woodblock (below).*

### DIARY 30 NOV (Th) 1871
Heard from Macmillan that they already have orders for 7500 *Looking-glasses* (they printed 9000), and are at once going to print 6000 more!

### DIARY 8 DEC (F) 1871
Received from Macmillan three *Looking-glasses* in morocco, and a hundred in cloth.

*To his uncle, Hassard Dodgson.*

#### CHRIST CHURCH, OXFORD
#### 14 MAY 1872

My dear Uncle,
    In writing 'The Walrus and the Carpenter,' I had no particular poem in my mind. The metre is a common one, and I don't think

'Eugene Aram' suggested it more than the many other poems I have read in the same metre.

'Sitting on a Gate', *is* a parody, though not as to style or metre — but its plot is borrowed from Wordsworth's 'Resolution and Independence,' a poem that has always amused me a good deal (though it is by no means a comic poem) by the absurd way in which the poet goes on questioning the poor old leech-gatherer, making him tell his history over and over again, and never attending to what he says. Wordsworth ends with a moral — an example I have *not* followed.

Ever your affectionate nephew,
C. L. Dodgson

*Later, in December that year, Dodgson wrote to Caroline Erskine, daughter of the Dean of Ripon, a woman some thirteen years older than himself.*

CHRIST CHURCH, OXFORD
15 DECEMBER 1872

Dear Miss Erskine,

. . . For myself, I am publishing nothing at present: the wells of my imagination soon run dry — besides, the *Looking-Glass* is having such a tremendous sale, it would be a pity to interfere with it. We have sold about 25000! . . .

Sincerely Yours,
C. L. Dodgson

If I find any more nice new books, I will send you word.

ABOVE: *The Walrus and the Carpenter. Dodgson originally suggested a carpenter, butterfly or baronet and left the final choice to Tenniel (each word fitted the scansion and he had no particular preference).*

ABOVE AND BELOW: *Tenniel's sketch (above) and final version (below) of the White Knight sliding down the poker, from* Through the Looking-Glass.

# The Snark

### 1873–1880

THE TWO *ALICE* books were established successes by the time Dodgson had the inspiration for his best-known other work, *The Hunting of the Snark*. On 17 July 1874, when staying at The Chestnuts, Guildford, he sat up most of the night with his cousin, Charlie Wilcox, who was dying from tuberculosis. He later described what happened the next day.

> I was walking on a hillside, alone, one bright summer day, when suddenly there came into my head one line of verse — one solitary line — 'For the Snark *was* a Boojum, you see.' I knew not what it meant, then; I know not what it means now: but I wrote it down: and some time afterwards, the rest of the stanza occurred to me, that being its last line: and so by degrees, at odd moments during the next year or two, the rest of the poem pieced itself together, that being its last stanza. And since then, periodically, I have received courteous letters from strangers, begging to know whether *The Hunting of the Snark* is an allegory, or contains some hidden moral, or is a political satire: and for all such questions I have but one answer, 'I don't know!'

He did agree it *could* be an allegory of the search for happiness:

> I think this fits it beautifully in many ways — particularly about the bathing-machines: when the people get weary of life, and can't find happiness in towns or in books, then they rush off to the seaside, to see what bathing-machines will do for them.

As for why that first inspired line came to him when it did, some commentators have suggested that it was a retreat into nonsense after

*Edith.*
*Sep. 14/80*

his distressing night with his sick cousin (Charlie Wilcox died less than four months later). But curious lines of verse must frequently have occurred to Dodgson and need no special explanation.

Meanwhile, in the 1870s, Dodgson's interest in little girls blossomed, and the number that he befriended grew and grew. As ever, he would amuse them with stories. Gertrude Chataway (whom he met on an Isle of Wight beach) described the charm of these:

> We used to sit for hours on the wooden steps which led from our garden onto the beach, whilst he told me the most lovely tales that could possibly be imagined, often illustrating the exciting situations with a pencil as he went along.
>
> One thing that made his stories particularly charming to a child was that he often took his cue from her remarks — a question would set him off on quite a new trail of ideas, so that one felt that one had somehow helped to make the story and it seemed a personal possession.

Or he would set them puzzles or sketch them or, when back at Oxford, photograph them. And when separated from them he would write to them. In part, his feelings were avuncular: like any favourite uncle, he enjoyed being loved by these little friends. But there are clear suggestions in his letters that with some he fell romantically in love. To Agnes Hull he wrote, 'My own Aggie though, when I think of all the pain you have given me, I feel inclined to put the syllables in another order and say "My Agg – own – ie."'

Many of these little friends were the daughters of fellow academics at Oxford. Others came from acting families, discovered when he saw them perform child roles. Others again he collected on train journeys or on the beaches of Sandown, on the Isle of Wight, or Eastbourne, the seaside resorts where he spent his summer vacations. The great majority were middle class, and none were from what he called 'peasant' stock — indeed, he once wrote that his personal idea of beauty would have made him exclude these as models because their ankles were too thick.

Sometimes he would photograph them in their normal clothes, but increasingly he liked to take them in theatrical costume, or in the nude. It would be naive to imagine that he got no pleasure from such sessions, and one explanation for Dodgson's obsession is that its pattern could have been set as a boy, when he perhaps fell in love with one of his little sisters.

Even though he could explain his obsession to himself as the pursuit of art, he was not insensitive to public opinion; but he refused to allow this to interfere with his conviction that he was behaving in a way in which, as an artist, he was perfectly entitled to behave.

It was probably because he found it difficult to persuade enough respectable parents to agree with him that he began to use professional child models. The person who was most helpful in providing him with these was Miss E. Gertrude Thomson, a woman of about thirty when he first made contact with her and a professional artist specializing in fairies. But he continued to prefer the children of friends; about a nude photographic session with Annie Henderson, daughter of a Fellow of Wadham, he wrote, 'She was worth any number of my models of yesterday.'

◆

*Helen Feilden was about thirteen when Dodgson wrote to her in March 1873. (The solution to the puzzle is that a second diamond-shaped window was constructed to fit inside the frame of the first.)*

### CHRIST CHURCH, OXFORD
### 15 MARCH 1873

My dear Helen,

 . . . I don't know if you are fond of puzzles, or not. If you are, try this. If not, never mind. A gentleman (a nobleman let us say, to make it more interesting) had a sitting-room with only one window in it — a

square window, 3 feet high and 3 feet wide. Now he had weak eyes, and the window gave too much light, *so* (don't you like '*so*' in a story?) he sent for the builder, and told him to alter it, so as only to give half the light. Only, he was to keep it square — he was to keep it 3 feet high — and he was to keep it 3 feet wide. How did he do it? Remember, he wasn't allowed to use curtains, or shutters, or coloured glass, or anything of that sort.

I must tell you an awful story of my trying to set a puzzle to a little girl the other day. It was at a dinner party, at dessert. I had never seen her before, but, as she was sitting next to me, I rashly proposed to her to try the puzzle (I daresay you know it) of 'the fox, and goose, and bag of corn.' And I got some biscuits to represent the fox and the other things. Her mother was sitting on the other side, and said, 'Now mind you take pains, my dear, and do it right!' The consequences were awful! She *shrieked* out, 'I can't do it! I can't do it! Oh, Mamma! Mamma!' threw herself into her mother's lap, and went off into a fit of sobbing which lasted several minutes! That was a lesson to me about trying children with puzzles. I do hope the square window won't produce any awful effect on *you*! I am

Your very affectionate friend,
C. L. Dodgson

BELOW: *Xie (Alexandra) Kitchin photographed as a Chinaman by Dodgson, who thought her 'the best way to secure* Excellence *in a photograph'. Xie's father, George William Kitchin, was a close friend and colleague of Dodgson's from their early days at Christ Church together.*

*Xie Kitchin (an abbreviation of Alexandra so presumably pronounced 'Exy') was the daughter of Dodgson's old friend, G. W. Kitchin, headmaster of Twyford School. By August 1873 he had been photographing her for four years in all manner of different costumes — 'gypsy-child', 'dressed in rags', 'Indian shawls', 'Winter dress (Danish)', 'Greek dress', 'Chinese dress'. Apart from Alice Liddell, she was his favourite sitter.*

### CHRIST CHURCH, OXFORD
### 21 AUGUST 1873

My dear Xie,

. . . The day after you went, I passed by your garden, and saw the little pug-dog wandering in and out, and it turned up its nose at me. So I went up to it and said, 'It is not good manners to turn up your nose at people!' Its eyes filled with tears, and it said, 'I wasn't doing it at *you*, Sir! It was only to keep myself from crying.' 'But what are you crying about, little pug-dog?' said I. The poor little dog rubbed its paws over its eyes, and said, 'Because my Ex —' 'Because your Extravagance has ruined you?' I said. 'Then let it be a lesson to you *not* to be extravagant. You should only spend a halfpenny a year.' 'No, it's *not* that,' said the little dog. 'It's because my Ex —' 'Because your Excellent master, Mr Kitchin, is gone?' I said. '*No!*' said the little dog. '*Do* let me finish the word! It's because my Exie is gone!' 'Well! What of that?' I said. 'She's only a child! She's not a bone!'

'No,' said the pug: 'she's not a bone.'

'Now, tell me the truth,' I said. 'Which do you like the best? Xie, or a bone?'

The little dog thought for a minute, and then he said, 'She's very "bonne," you know: that means "good" in French. But she's not so good as a bone!'

Wasn't it an interesting conversation? . . .

Yours very affectionately,
C. L. Dodgson

*Dodgson continued to be troubled by his stammer. In September 1873 he had consulted H. F. Rivers about 'my difficulties with "p" in such combinations as "impossible"', frustrated that 'the hope I had formed of being very soon able to help in Church again' was quashed. In December, he wrote to him again.*

### CHRIST CHURCH, OXFORD
### 19 DECEMBER 1873

My dear Rivers,

. . . Just now I am in a bad way for speaking, and a good deal discouraged. I actually so entirely broke down, twice lately, over a hard 'C', that I had to spell the word! Once was in a shop, which made it more annoying; however it is an annoyance one must make up one's mind to bear, I suppose, now and then — especially when, as now, I have been rather hard worked . . .

Very truly yours,
C. L. Dodgson

*To H. F. Rivers*

### THE CHESTNUTS, GUILDFORD
### 27 DECEMBER 1873

My dear Rivers,

. . . Thanks for advice about hard 'C', which I acknowledge as my vanquisher in single-hand combat, at present. As to working the jaw more, your advice is within my power, generally: but as to the direction to 'keep the back of the tongue down,' *in the moment of difficulty*, I fear you might almost as well advise me to stand on my head! Believe me

Very truly yours,
C. L. Dodgson

BELOW: *Sketch by Dodgson in a letter to Xie Kitchin of February 1880, suggesting that by the time he next sees her she may have grown too tall for him to photograph attractively. 'Please don't grow any taller—if you can help it,' he asked her.*

*Dodgson's stammer was by no means unique in his family.*

**CHRIST CHURCH, OXFORD**
**2 FEBRUARY 1874**

My dear Rivers,

The state of the case regarding my sisters is this. There are 7 in all.

1 does not stammer.

2 stammer very slightly (of these one is such an invalid, you are not likely ever to see her).

2 stammer to a moderate amount (of those one is married and lives in the north of England — you will never see *her*).

2 stammer rather badly.

So that probably you might have coming to you for lessons *two* rather bad cases, *one* moderate, and *one* very slight. If with this prospect (plus myself for occasional lessons), you are willing to take 30 guineas as fair remuneration, I have much pleasure in closing with the offer — and I enclose a cheque to the amount . . .

Sincerely yours,
C. L. Dodgson

*Gaynor and Amy Simpson were little girls whom Dodgson admired chiefly for their acting. In his diary for 2 January 1873 he wrote that 'Gaynor's Cinderella was a thing to be remembered.'*

**THE CHESTNUTS, GUILDFORD**
**27 DECEMBER 1873**

My dear Gaynor,

. . . As to dancing, my dear, I *never* dance, unless I am allowed to do it *in my own peculiar way*. There is no use trying to describe it: it has to be seen to be believed. The last house I tried it in, the floor broke through. But then it was a poor sort of floor — the beams were only six inches thick, hardly worth calling beams at all: stone arches are much more sensible, when any dancing, *of my peculiar kind*, is to be done. Did you ever see the Rhinoceros, and the Hippopotamus, at the Zoological Gardens, trying to dance a minuet together? It is a touching sight.

Give any message from me to Amy that you think will be most likely to surprise her, and believe me

Your affectionate friend,
Lewis Carroll

◆

*Dodgson first met the Marquis of Salisbury when he was installed as Chancellor of the University at Oxford in June 1870. Now, in December 1874, he was invited to stay at Salisbury's ancestral home, Hatfield House in Hertfordshire. From there he finished off a letter to Maud Standen, which he had begun while still in Guildford. Maud, now about seventeen, was the daughter of a well-known Indian Army family, chanced upon by Dodgson on Oxford Railway Station in 1869.*

### THE CHESTNUTS, GUILDFORD
### 30 DECEMBER 1874

My dear Maud,

I came yesterday, to be present at a children's fancy ball, which was a very pretty sight. The house is Elizabethan, so most of the dresses were of that period: the eldest girl, Maud, being dressed as Queen Elizabeth, and the ball began with a grand royal procession, which was very well done — a little page to carry her train, and a little Lord Chamberlain with a long wand to walk backwards before her. Then they had a morris-dance, holding ribbons

BELOW: *Main staircase at Hatfield House, family home of the Salisburys. On a visit, Dodgson began to expand his Sylvie and* Bruno *stories by telling them to the Marquis's daughters. 'The appetite of the party for stories is insatiable,' he wrote in his diary.*

BELOW: *Dodgson's portrait of the Marquis of Salisbury, at his installation as Chancellor of the University of Oxford, with his two sons, James and William.*

from one to another, and then the regular dancing began. There were about 100 children altogether: they had a supper at 9½ and *another* supper at 12! This was only for the people staying in the house, about 40 people, including about 20 children. I took my drawing-book into the gallery during the ball, and drew a picture of a little Amy Robsart, who consented to stand still for a few minutes . . .

Your ever affectionate friend,
C. L. Dodgson

*Meanwhile, in the summer of 1874, he had made the visit to The Chestnuts, Guildford, during which that single inspired line, which began the writing of* The Hunting of the Snark, *occurred to him. A year later he met Gertrude Chataway on the beach at Sandown. When* The Snark *was published its dedication took the form of an acrostic, the letters of Gertrude's name starting its sixteen lines.*

### CHRIST CHURCH, OXFORD
### 13 OCTOBER 1875

My dear Gertrude,

I never give birthday *presents*, but you see I *do* sometimes write a birthday letter . . . I am writing this to wish you many and many a happy return of your birthday tomorrow. I will drink your health, if only I can remember, and if you don't mind — but perhaps you object? You see, if I were to sit by you at breakfast, and to drink your tea, you wouldn't like *that*, would you? You would say 'Boo! hoo! Here's Mr Dodgson's drunk all my tea, and I haven't got any left!' So I am very much afraid, next time Sybil looks for you, she'll find you sitting by the sad sea wave, and crying 'Boo! hoo! Here's Mr Dodgson has drunk my health, and I haven't got any left!' And how it will puzzle Dr Maund, when he is sent for to see you! 'My dear Madam, I'm very sorry to say your little girl has got *no health at all*! I never saw such a thing in my life!' 'Oh, I can easily explain it!' your Mother will say. 'You see she *would* go and make friends with a strange gentleman, and yesterday he drank her health!'

ABOVE: *Dodgson's sketch of Gertrude Chataway in fisherman's jersey and cap.*

RIGHT: *Gertrude Chataway as photographed by Dodgson. He met her at Sandown in 1875 and she soon became his favourite little friend. It was to her that he dedicated* The Hunting of the Snark, *in the form of an acrostic which began,* 'Girt with a boyish garb for boyish task,/Eager she wields her spade; yet loves as well/Rest on a friendly knee, intent to ask/The tale he loves to tell.'

LEFT: *View of Ventnor, not far from Sandown Bay on the southeast coast of the Isle of Wight, where Dodgson spent many summer vacations before 1877 and where he met many of his young friends, including Gertrude Chataway.*

'Well, Mrs Chataway,' he will say, 'the only way to cure her is to wait till his next birthday, and then for *her* to drink *his* health.'

And then we shall have changed healths. I wonder how you'll like mine! Oh Gertrude, I wish you wouldn't talk such nonsense! . . .

And now with best love and half-a-dozen kisses for yourself, I remain

Your loving friend,
Lewis Carroll

*To Mrs Chataway, Gertrude's mother, about* The Hunting of the Snark, *a weird tale in which a handful of adults (whose names all begin with 'B') set off to capture the mythical Snark, in a ship that will only sail backwards.*

CHRIST CHURCH, OXFORD
7 NOVEMBER 1875

Dear Mrs Chataway,

With the exception of my Publisher, Printer, and Artist, and my own family, I have told nobody yet of my intention of bringing out a little Christmas book. And I think *you* are the next person to whom the announcement ought to be made, because I have taken, as a dedication, the verses I sent you the other day in MS. It will be a very small book — not 40 pages — a poem (supposed to be comic) with a frontispiece by Mr Holiday. The advertisements will appear about the middle of this month, I suppose, and till then I should be glad if you would not let the *name* of the book go beyond your own family-circle. I don't mind the fact, that the book is in the press, being known — but the name ought to be *new* when it appears. It is called *The Hunting of the Snark*, and the scene is laid in an island frequented by the Jubjub and Bandersnatch — no doubt the very island in which the Jabberwock was slain (see *Through the Looking-Glass*) . . .

Yours very sincerely,
C. L. Dodgson

I send love, and a kiss, to Gertrude . . .

111

*Delays meant* The Hunting of the Snark *did not appear until
1 April 1876. Florence (Birdie) Balfour was the daughter of a stockbroker,
met, like other little friends, on Sandown beach, Isle of Wight.*

### CHRIST CHURCH, OXFORD
### 6 APRIL 1876

My dear Birdie,

When you have read the *Snark*, I hope you will write me a little
note and tell me how you like it, and if you can *quite* understand it.
Some children are puzzled with it. Of course you know what a Snark
is? If you do, please tell *me*: for I haven't an idea what it is like. And
tell me which of the pictures you like best.

Your affectionate friend,
Lewis Carroll

*Gertrude Chataway continued to be his favourite little friend. Writing
to her mother in June 1876, he added a postscript.*

### CHRIST CHURCH, OXFORD
### 28 JUNE 1876

P.S. If you should decide on sending over Gertrude and not coming
yourself, would you kindly let me know what is the minimum amount
of dress in which you are willing to have her taken? With that
information, I will then be guided by *her* likings in the matter:
children differ very much — with some that I know (Londoners
chiefly) I would not venture to propose even taking off their shoes:
but with a child like your Gertrude, as simple-minded as Eve in the
garden of Eden, *I* should see no objection (provided she liked it
herself) to photographing her in Eve's original dress. And I think, if
you were here and could see the photographs I have done of children
in that primitive costume, that you would agree that it is quite
possible to make such a picture that you might frame it and hang it up
in your drawing-room.

RIGHT: *'But oh, beamish nephew, beware of the day,/If your Snark be a Boojum! For then/You will softly and suddenly vanish away,/And never be met with again!'* *Illustration by Henry Holiday for* The Hunting of the Snark. *Dodgson denied that he knew what the poem meant, but when pressed said that it could be read as an allegory of the search for happiness.*

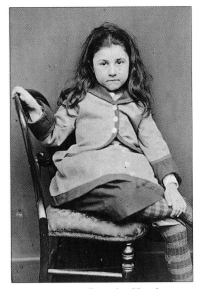

ABOVE: *Beatrice Hatch,*
*photographed by Dodgson.*

*Dodgson had photographed Beatrice (Birdie) Hatch naked in July*
*1873. Now, nearly four years later, he wrote to her mother,*
*asking a favour.*

CHRIST CHURCH, OXFORD
14 MARCH 1877

Dear Mrs Hatch,

You know that photo I did of Birdie, seated in a crouching attitude, side view, with one hand to her chin, in the days before she had learned to consider dress as *de rigueur*? It was a gem the equal of which I have not much hope of doing again: and I should very much like, if possible, to get Miss Bond, of Southsea (the best photographic colourist living, *I* think) to colour a copy. But I am shy of asking her the question, people have such different views, and it *might* be a shock to her feelings if I did so. *Would* you kindly do it for me? . . .

Sincerely yours,
C. L. Dodgson

*Mrs Blakemore was the mother of five-year-old 'Dolly,' met on*
*2 August at Eastbourne, which Dodgson had that year substituted for*
*Sandown as his seaside holiday place. He continued to spend summers*
*there for the rest of his life.*

7 LUSHINGTON ROAD, EASTBOURNE
13 AUGUST 1877

Dear Mrs Blakemore,

They have a custom in Russia, when a young man has paid his addresses to a young lady, and when the parents, not approving the match, wish to give the young man a hint to go about his business, of sending the said young man a basket of flowers and fruit: and the friends of the young man smile maliciously, and say, 'He is basketed,' or 'He has got his basket,' which is equivalent to saying, 'He has been properly snubbed.' If I thought *that* was the meaning of your kind

RIGHT: *Watercolour of Beatrice (Birdie) Hatch by Anne Lydia Bond, copied from one of Dodgson's photographs. The colouring of this nude portrait by 'Miss Bond, of Southsea' was discussed in a letter to Birdie's mother dated 14 March 1877 (opposite page). Dodgson was a friend of the Hatch family for over twenty-five years. The father, Edwin, was a controversial theologian. In 1933, Beatrice's sister, Evelyn, published a selection of Dodgson's letters.*

gift, I should be strongly tempted to return it indignantly and say, 'Not all the flowers and fruit in England are worth Dolly's love' — but feeling that it is *not* meant as a substitute for *that*, I am gratefully consuming it . . .

I hope you will soon pay me a visit: I will be in *any* hour and *any* day, that you like to name. Literally I have *no* engagements at all.

Sincerely yours,
C. L. Dodgson

LEFT: *Young girls paddling at Yarmouth, one of many typical and enduring sights of the seaside.* 'Alice had been to the seaside once in her life, and had come to the general conclusion that, wherever you go to on the English coast, you find a number of bathing machines in the sea, some children digging in the sand with wooden spades, then a row of lodging houses, and behind them a railway station.' Alice's Adventures in Wonderland

*To an unknown child met at Eastbourne the same summer*

Oh child, child! I kept my promise yesterday afternoon, and came down to the sea, to go with you along the rocks: but I saw you going with another gentleman, so I thought I wasn't wanted just yet: so I walked about a bit, and when I got back I couldn't see you anywhere, though I went a good way on the rocks to look. There *was* a child in pink that looked [like] you; but when I got up to her it was the wrong child: however that wasn't *her* fault, poor thing. She couldn't help being a stranger. So I helped her with her sand-castles, and then I went home. I didn't cry *all* the way.

Your loving friend,
C. L. Dodgson

*Agnes Hull was the twelve-year-old daughter of a lawyer, met at Eastbourne the previous August. She became one of his favourite little friends.*

### CHRIST CHURCH, OXFORD
#### 10 DECEMBER 1877

My dear Agnes,

At *last* I've succeeded in forgetting you! It's been a very hard job, but I took 6 'lessons-in-forgetting,' at half-a-crown a lesson. After three lessons, I forgot my own name, and I forgot to go for the next lesson. So the Professor said I was getting on very well: 'but I hope,' he added, 'you won't forget to pay for the lessons!' I said *that* would depend on whether the other lessons were good or not: and do you know? the last of the 6 lessons was so good that I forgot *everything*! I forgot who I was: I forgot to eat my dinner: and, so far, I've quite forgotten to pay the man. I will give you his address, as perhaps you would like to take lessons from him, so as to forget *me*. He lives in the middle of Hyde Park, and his name is 'Mr Gnome Emery.' It *is* such a comfort to have forgotten all about Agnes, and Evey, and — and — and I feel as happy as the day is short! (I would have said 'as the day is *long*,' only, you see, this is winter, not summer.)

Oh, child, child! Why have you never been over to Oxford to be photographed? . . . What's the use of having a grown-up sister, if she can't escort you about England? . . .

Your loving friend,
Lewis Carroll

LEFT AND RIGHT: *Dodgson bought this painting of 'The Lady with the Lilacs' (left) from its artist, Arthur Hughes. It bears a striking resemblance to his own drawing of Alice (right) in the original manuscript of* Alice's Adventures Under Ground. *Although the pose of the two girls is similar, Alice's situation is much less romantic —* 'she found her head pressing against the ceiling, and she stooped to save her neck from being broken'!

ainst the ceiling, and she stooped to
r neck from being broken, and h
saying to herself
quite a
I hope I
grow any
I wish I
drunk so
Alas
was too
she wen
growing
growing,
soon had
kneel d
even

, and she tried **the** effect of
n, with one elbow against the

*Twelve-year-old Jessie Sinclair was the daughter of an actor, his
stage name Joseph Scrivener.*

### CHRIST CHURCH, OXFORD
### 22 JANUARY 1878

My dear Jessie,

I liked your letter better than anything I have had for some time.
I may as well just tell you a few of the things I like, and then,
whenever you want to give me a birthday present (my birthday comes
once every seven years, on the fifth Tuesday in April) you will know
what to give me. Well, I like, *very* much indeed, a little mustard with
a bit of beef spread thinly under it; and I like brown sugar — only it
should have some apple pudding mixed with it to keep it from being
too sweet; but perhaps what I like best of all is salt, with some soup
poured over it. The use of the soup is to hinder the salt from being too
dry; and it helps to melt it. Then there are other things I like; for
instance, pins — only they should always have a cushion put round
them to keep them warm. And I like two or three handfuls of hair;
only they should always have a little girl's head beneath them to grow
on, or else whenever you open the door they get blown all over the
room, and then they get lost, you know . . .

I think I'll come and see you again — suppose we say once every
two years; and in about ten years I really think we shall be good
friends. Don't you think we shall?

I shall be very glad to hear from you whenever you feel inclined
to write . . .

Your affectionate friend,
Lewis Carroll

*Mrs Henderson's husband, Patrick, was a Fellow of Wadham
College, Oxford, the first to be elected from outside the College, and one
of the first married tutors in Oxford. The Hendersons had three
daughters: Annie, Hamilton Frances and Lilian, who seems to have*

*been the most photogenic. According to her nephew, she 'was one of the most beautiful women I have ever seen, and this was borne out by those who had known her when a young girl at Oxford.'*

ABOVE: *Emily Gertrude Thomson, best known as an illustrator of fairies and fantasy. She became one of Dodgson's few adult women friends, and introduced him to a range of child models. A friend of Dodgson's told her, 'Mr Dodgson doesn't think of you as a "young lady" ... he looks upon you as a sort of "old child."'*

CHRIST CHURCH, OXFORD
20 JULY 1879

Dear Mrs Henderson,

Miss E. G. Thomson, the artist-friend I told you of, comes to me tomorrow, to spend the day: and I'm sure she would thoroughly enjoy helping to arrange the children for a few photographs, if they would like to come. If they themselves are *quite* willing to come, and if her presence will not make them shy of being undressed, I should be very glad if they could be left here at about 11 . . .

It is very pleasant to me to think that the children are so absolutely at their ease with me, and I assure you I take it as a great compliment and privilege that you are willing to trust me with them so entirely. I have never seen anything more beautiful in childhood than their *perfect* simplicity.

Sincerely yours,
C. L. Dodgson

◆

*To Mrs Henderson*

CHRIST CHURCH, OXFORD
31 MAY 1880

Dear Mrs Henderson,

I do hope you did not think I had taken a step not warranted by the circumstances, in allowing the children to live for 3 hours in their favorite costume, up in the studio. But I felt so confident that, when you told Annie they must not be taken naked because it was too cold, it was your *only* reason, that I thought that objection cleared away by the fact that the studio was, I should think, at nearer 80° than 70°.

Their innocent unconsciousness is very beautiful, and gives one a feeling of reverence, as at the presence of something sacred: and if

RIGHT: *One of E. Gertrude Thomson's drawings of fairies for Dodgson's* Three Sunsets and Other Poems. *She drew fairies in much the same style as he liked to photograph children.*

you had only those two girls, I should see no objection (in spite of 'Mrs Grundy') in their repeating the performance, if they wished, next year, or even for 2 or 3 years to come. But, for the sake of their little brother, I quite think you may find it desirable to bring such habits to an end after this summer. A boy's head soon imbibes precocious ideas, which might be a cause of unhappiness in future years . . .

Very sincerely yours,
C. L. Dodgson

# Sylvie and Bruno

### JULY 1880–JANUARY 1898

I N 1880 DODGSON'S LIFE underwent a change which it is not easy to explain. From July onwards he took no more photographs — though in September he suggested a sitting to the parents of one little friend, and he also continued to draw small girls in the nude. It was about this time that wet plate photography began to give way to dry plate, a technique which he considered inferior. But it is difficult to avoid believing that what really drove him to abandon a hobby which had been so important to him was a sense of public disapproval of the subjects he chose to photograph.

Writing now became his main occupation, and in 1881, to give himself even more time, he resigned his Christ Church lectureship. He planned to write in the causes of 'mathematical education', 'religious thought' and 'innocent recreation for children'. In 1885 a list of his current projects included seven books on mathematics or logic, two of games or puzzles, and seven of various other kinds. One of the latter was *Sylvie and Bruno*, his last great work of children's fiction (apart from its sequel, *Sylvie and Bruno Concluded*), which was eventually published in 1889.

Dodgson had been expanding his original story, 'Bruno's Revenge', published in *Aunt Judy's Magazine* in 1867, at least since January 1873 when, on a visit to the Salisbury family at Hatfield, the two Salisbury daughters, Maud and Gwendolen, demanded more Bruno stories. In his diary he wrote, 'I gave them a new chapter of Sylvie and Bruno ... which I must write out before I forget it,' and next day, 'the appetite of the party for stories is insatiable. Luckily I had thought of a few more incidents for Sylvie and Bruno, and gave them another chapter, which took nearly an hour.' From then onwards he had 'jotted down, at odd moments, all sorts of odd ideas and fragments of dialogue that occurred to me — who knows how?'

ABOVE: *Sketch by Dodgson for his poem, 'A Game of Fives'. 'In the foreground,' he explained, 'the father is saying, "Tell me what you mean!"' in an effort to secure a marriage proposal for at least one of his five daughters.*

*Each in his mouth a living Herring bore*

Eventually the first volume appeared in 1889, and the second in 1893, just five years before his death. Though he had put so much more effort into these than into the *Alice* books, they have never had the same success. He consciously intended them to be not merely 'a réchauffé of Alice'. One unfortunate consequence was that, while *Alice* had been intended only to amuse, into *Sylvie and Bruno* he introduced 'some thoughts...not wholly out of harmony with the graver cadences of Life.'

Meanwhile he had turned his ever active and inventive mind to a wide variety of other matters, including his elaborate proposals for fairer *Lawn Tennis Tournaments*, as his pamphlet on the subject was called, and suggestions (also in pamphlet form) for fairer voting arrangements at parliamentary elections. He had also campaigned to have the starving people of Tristan da Cunha (where his brother Edwin was a missionary) evacuated to Australia. And he had bought a primitive tricycle, known as a velociman, on which to cycle about the town, so confirming his reputation as the Oxford eccentric he was now becoming.

If his curatorship of the Christ Church Common Room, which he held for nine years, was a more conventional activity, he could not avoid treating it with a mock-innocent logic reminiscent of Alice's. After a year in which none of the inferior Madeira (B) had been drunk he calculated that the stock would last indefinitely and added, 'although there may be something monotonous and dreary in the prospect of such vast cycles spent in drinking second-class Madeira, we may cheer ourselves with the thought of how economically it may be done.'

In 1886 his continuing interest in the *Alice* books (various new editions had been published, including a facsimile of the original manuscript of *Alice's Adventures Under Ground* with his own illustrations) and his lifelong interest in the theatre came together when *Alice* was staged as an operetta. He befriended several of the girls in the casts of its various productions, and he also campaigned for longer holidays and better education for stage children.

During his last five years he published various mathematical books and books of puzzles, but *Sylvie and Bruno* remained his last imaginative work of any consequence. He died of bronchitis at the family home in Guildford on 14 January 1898, aged sixty-six. His books had earned him considerable sums, but he left only just over £4,000, evidence of his unfailing generosity to family and friends. He was generous in other ways too. His last piece of published writing was a contribution to a book for children, *The Lost Plum-Cake*, by his cousin, Georgie Wilcox. The fact that Dodgson had supplied the final chapter was only revealed thirty years later.

ABOVE: *Advertisement for the first stage performance of the operetta 'Alice in Wonderland' at London's Prince of Wales's Theatre in 1886.*

RIGHT: *A Victorian audience emerges from a pantomime matinée performance of 1865. The little girls all seem to bear an uncanny resemblance to 'Alice'.*

---

*Dodgson's relationship with Agnes Hull had now lasted four years and was reaching its most painful period.*

CHRIST CHURCH, OXFORD
21 APRIL 1881

My darling Aggie,
    (Oh yes, I know quite well what you're saying — 'Why can't the man take a *hint*? He might have *seen* that the beginning of my last

Why, how can she know that no harm has
gazing at it for hours together with
for instance, the number of beetles
myself 'your loving' you g
then I go down another
truly, Lewis Carroll'.
Oct. 22/78

LEFT: *Circular letter from Dodgson
to Agnes Hull, dated 22 October
1878. Dodgson first met and
photographed Agnes and two of her
sisters at Eastbourne in 1877. She
subsequently became one of his most
frequent correspondents, in spite of
occasional complaints from Dodgson
that she was stand-offish.*

letter was meant to show that my affection was cooling down!' Why, of course I saw it! But is that any reason why *mine* should cool down, to match? I put it to you as a reasonable young person — one who, from always arguing with Alice for an hour before getting up, has had good practice in Logic — haven't I a right to be affectionate if I like? Surely, just as much as *you* have to be as unaffectionate as *you* like. And of course you mustn't think of *writing* a bit more than you *feel*: no, no, *truth* before all things!) (Cheers. Ten minutes allowed for refreshment.) I came up to town on Monday with Mr Sampson (some of you have met him at Eastborne) to see *The Cup* and *The Belle's Stratagem*, and on Tuesday I made a call or two before going back to Guildford, and passed High Street, Kensington. I had turned it (half) over in (half of) my mind, the idea of calling at 55. But Common Sense said, 'No. Aggie will only tease you by offering you the extremity of her left ear to kiss, and will say, "This is for the *last* time, Mr Dodgson, because I'm going to be sixteen next month!"' 'Don't you know,' said Common Sense, 'that *last times* of anything are very unpleasant? Better avoid it, and wait till her sixteenth birthday is over:

BELOW AND RIGHT: *Illustrations at the side of Dodgson's letter to Marion Richards of October 1881. Their friendship 'began so awfully quick,' he told her, 'that it's pretty sure to end off just as suddenly'— before long they would be on bowing terms, 'just when we happen to see each other at opposite sides of the street.'*

then you'll be on shaking-hands terms, which will be calm and comfortable.' 'You are right, Common Sense,' said I. 'I'll go and call on other young ladies.' . . .

Your loving friend,
C. L. D.

*Eleven-year-old Marion Richards, another of his Eastbourne little friends, was the daughter of a surgeon. Her mother, a widow, gave a home to children whose parents were serving in India.*

CHRIST CHURCH, OXFORD
26 OCTOBER 1881

My dear little Girl,
(There! I don't think I ever began a letter like that before . . .
*Marion* '— and you'd better never begin another so: it would be much prettier to put "Marion" than "Girl".'
*Me* 'I don't think so: it rhymes to "pearl" and "curl", and the other only rhymes to "Bulgarian"!'
But of course I shall soon have to alter it: you see our friendship began so *awfully* quick — quite dangerous, it was so sudden — almost like a railway-accident: that it's pretty sure to end off just as suddenly. Next year, I suppose, we shall have got to shaking-hands terms, and the year after that we shall be on bowing terms, just when we happen to see each other at opposite sides of the street.) . . .

Always your loving friend,
C. L. Dodgson

*Florence (Birdie) Balfour was now about eleven.*

CHRIST CHURCH, OXFORD
10 FEBRUARY 1882

My dear Birdie,
As are the feelings of the old lady who, after feeding her canary and going out for a walk, finds the cage entirely filled, on her return,

with a live turkey — or of the old gentleman who, after chaining up a small terrier overnight, finds a hippopotamus raging around the kennel in the morning — such are my feelings when, trying to recall the memory of a small child who used to wade in the sea at Sandown, I meet with the astonishing photograph of the same microcosm suddenly expanded into a tall young person, whom I should be too shy to look at, even with a telescope which would no doubt be necessary to get any distinct idea of her smile, or at any rate, to satisfy oneself whether she has eyebrows or not!

There! that long sentence has exhausted me, and I have only strength to say 'thank you' very sincerely, for the 2 photographs. They are terribly lifelike!

Are you going to be at Sandown next Summer? It is just *possible* I may be running over there for 2 or 3 days: but Eastbourne is always my headquarters now. Believe me

Yours affectionately,
C. L. Dodgson

◆

*A Shakespeare for girls was one of the projects on Dodgson's 1885 list. Three years earlier he had written to Mrs Richards, mother of Marion, a child friend, on the subject.*

CHRIST CHURCH, OXFORD
13 MARCH 1882

Dear Mrs Richards,

... Are you a Shakespeare reader? I have a dream of Bowdlerising Bowdler, i.e. of editing a Shakespeare which shall be absolutely fit for *girls*. For this I need advice, from *mothers*, as to which plays they would like to be included. Could you put down for me the names of those you think might be made good reading for girls (from 10 to 20 years old, let us say).

Best love to Marion.

Sincerely yours,
C. L. Dodgson

*To whom this letter, probably written in 1882, was addressed is not known.*

... I doubt if I am fully a 'High Churchman' now. I find that as life slips away (I am over fifty now), and the life on the other side of the great river becomes more and more the reality, of which *this* is only a shadow, that the pretty distinctions of the many creeds of Christendom tend to slip away as well — leaving only the great truths which all Christians believe alike. More and more, as I read of the Christian religion, as Christ preached it, I stand amazed at the forms men have given to it, and the fictitious barriers they have built up between themselves and their brethren...

♦

*Dodgson became Curator of Christ Church Common Room in December 1882, with responsibility, among other things, for its wine cellar. Early the next year, he wrote to the wine merchants Messrs Barrett & Clay for advice.*

### CHRIST CHURCH, OXFORD
### 25 JANUARY 1883

The Curator of the Common Room (the Rev. C. L. Dodgson) will be much obliged if Messrs Barret & Clay would give him the benefit of their advice on 2 or 3 points in the treatment of wine, about which he finds much difference of opinion to exist.
(1) What amount of damp is desirable in a wine-cellar?
(2) Is ventilation desirable?
(3) Should light be admitted?

He would also thank them if they would fill in the enclosed paper, as to particular temperatures needed, etc...

ABOVE: *Portrait of Dodgson taken in his later years. For nine of these years he was the Curator of the Christ Church Senior Common Room, with responsibility for, among other things, its cellar.*

*Dodgson's letter to Oscar Fay Adams was not the first attempt he had made to get himself excluded from a biographical dictionary.*

### 7 SEPTEMBER 1883

Mr Lewis Carroll will feel very grateful to Mr Oscar Fay Adams if he will kindly abandon his intention of including his name in the dictionary he is preparing.

Mr Carroll has the greatest dislike to personal publicity of any kind, which is his reason for writing under a pseudonym.

*One brief letter and a fragment of another to Alice Liddell, now Mrs Hargreaves, survive from 1883. The many earlier ones he had written her were all destroyed by Mrs Liddell — one of the more regrettable acts of literary vandalism. He now wrote again.*

### CHRIST CHURCH, OXFORD
### 1 MARCH 1885

My dear Mrs Hargreaves,

I fancy this will come to you almost like a voice from the dead, after so many years of silence — and yet those years have made no difference, that I can perceive, in *my* clearness of memory of the days when we *did* correspond. I am getting to feel what an old man's failing memory is, as to recent events and new friends (for instance, I made friends, only a few weeks ago, with a very nice little maid of about 12, and had a walk with her — and now I can't recall either of her names!) but my mental picture is as vivid as ever, of one who was, through so many years, my ideal child-friend. I have had scores of child-friends since your time: but they have been quite a different thing.

However, I did not begin this letter to say all *that*. What I want to ask is — would you have any objection to the original MS book of *Alice's Adventures* (which I suppose you still possess) being published in facsimile? The idea of doing so occurred to me only the other day. If, on consideration, you come to the conclusion that you would rather *not* have it done, there is an end of the matter. If, however, you give a favorable reply, I would be much obliged if you would lend it me (registered post I should think would be safest) that I may consider the possibilities. I have not seen it for about 20 years: so am by no means sure that the illustrations may not prove to be so awfully bad, that to reproduce them would be absurd.

There can be no doubt that I should incur the charge of gross egoism in publishing it. But I don't care for that in the least: knowing that I have no such motive: only I think, considering the extraordinary popularity the books have had (we have sold more than 120,000 of the two) there must be many who would like to see the original form.

Always your friend,
C. L. Dodgson

*The photograph which Dodgson mentions in his next letter to Mrs Hargreaves was of Alice when she was seven. He had pasted it at the end of the manuscript of* Alice's Adventures Under Ground. *When it was eventually removed it revealed a drawing of her, which had presumably not satisfied him. But nor did the photograph now please him, and it was not used in Macmillan's 1886 facsimile edition.*

### CHRIST CHURCH, OXFORD
### 7 MARCH 1885

My dear Mrs Hargreaves,

Many thanks for your permission. The greatest care shall be taken of the MS (I am gratified at your making *that* a condition!). My own wishes would be distinctly *against* reproducing the photograph.

Always your friend,
C. L. Dodgson

ABOVE AND RIGHT: *On the final page of* Alice's Adventures Under Ground, *which he gave Alice Liddell in 1864, Dodgson concealed his drawing of her (above) with a photograph (right).*

*To prepare this edition, Dodgson employed a certain Mr Noad, whom Macmillan had recommended. He wrote to tell Mrs Hargreaves of the problems this had caused.*

ABOVE: *'Who Stole the Tarts?'*
*Tenniel's illustration of the trial*
*scene in* Alice's Adventures in
Wonderland, *as coloured for* The
Nursery 'Alice'.

### CHRIST CHURCH, OXFORD
### 11 NOVEMBER 1886

My dear Mrs Hargreaves,

... Mr Noad did a first-rate set of negatives, and took them away with him to get the zinc-blocks made. These he delivered pretty regularly at first, and there seemed to be every prospect of getting the book out by Christmas 1885 ... Soon after this — I having prepaid for the whole of the zinc-blocks — the supply suddenly ceased, while *22* pages were still due, and Mr Noad disappeared!

My belief is that he was in hiding from his creditors. We sought him in vain. So things went on for months. At one time I thought of employing a detective to find him, but was assured that 'all detectives are scoundrels.' ... In April he called at Macmillan's and left *8* blocks, and again vanished into obscurity.

This left us with 14 pages (dotted up and down the book) still missing. I waited a while longer, and then put the thing into the hands of a Solicitor, who soon found the man, but could get nothing but promises from him. 'You will never get the blocks,' said the Solicitor, 'unless you frighten him by a summons before a Magistrate.' To this at last I unwillingly consented; the summons had to be taken out at Stratford-le-Bow (that is where this aggravating man is living), and this entailed 2 journeys from Eastbourne — one to get the summons (my *personal* presence being necessary), and the other to attend in Court with the Solicitor on the day fixed for hearing the case. The defendant didn't appear; so the Magistrate said he would take the case in his absence. Then I had the new and exciting experience of being put into the witness-box, and sworn, and cross-examined by a rather savage Magistrate's clerk, who seemed to think that, if he only bullied me enough, he would soon catch me out in a falsehood! I had to give the Magistrate a little lecture on photo-zincography, and the poor man declared the case was so complicated he must adjourn it for another week. But this time, in order to secure the presence of our slippery defendant, he issued a warrant for his apprehension, and the constable had orders to take him into custody and lodge him in prison,

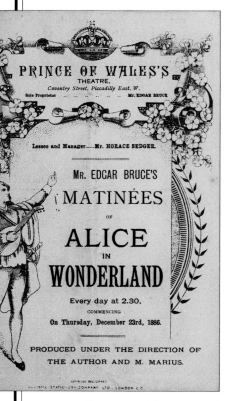

ABOVE: *Programme (first page and back page advertisement) for the first stage performance of 'Alice in Wonderland', a musical play which, in spite of its name, was based on both the* Alice *books.*

the night before the day when the case was to come on. The news of *this* effectually frightened him, and he delivered up the 14 negatives (he hadn't done the blocks) before the fatal day arrived . . .

Sincerely yours,
C. L. Dodgson

*Henry Savile Clarke was a playwright, critic and newspaper editor. On 28 August 1886 he wrote to Dodgson asking for permission to make the* Alice *books into an operetta. Dodgson gave his consent but kept a close watch on the proceedings.*

7 LUSHINGTON ROAD, EASTBOURNE
30 AUGUST 1886

Dear Sir,

There is one, and only one, condition which I should regard as absolutely *essential* before allowing my name to appear as 'sanctioning' any dramatic version of *Alice in Wonderland* or *Through the Looking-Glass*. There are one or two *wishes* on the subject, which I will name for your consideration: but the only essential condition is that I should have your written guarantee that, neither in the libretto nor in any of the stage business, shall any coarseness, or anything suggestive of coarseness, be admitted . . .

May I ask you *not* to give any publicity to my real name? *Personal* publicity I dislike greatly, and avoid it as much as possible . . .

Truly yours,
C. L. Dodgson

*To Henry Savile Clarke*

THE CHESTNUTS, GUILDFORD
31 OCTOBER 1886

Dear Mr Savile Clarke,

. . . I have two small requests to make, as to the drama, which I hope the author may not unfairly make. One, to erase 'What are tarts

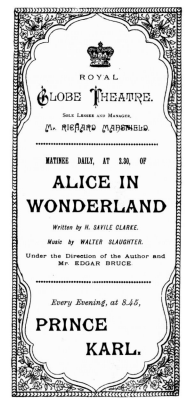

ABOVE: *The operetta was restaged at the Globe two years later. Dodgson was not impressed: 'The White King fell flat on his back with his feet towards the audience, who . . . were thus presented with a view of him which I leave to your imagination.'*

made of?' and to substitute the following 'business.' Enter Cook, carrying a large soup-tureen, with a ladle: she pushes her way round the Court, and, wherever she goes, those around her are in fits of sneezing — the fits beginning suddenly, as soon as she is within 2 yards of any one, and ceasing as suddenly, when she has passed by. (I think that great tidal wave of sneezing might be rather funny.) Then the King asks (and the question comes in quite naturally):

'What's that soup made of?'

'Pepper, mostly.'

'Treacle!' says the Dormouse.

My second small request is that the Hatter may *drawl*, not *hesitate*, with long pauses between the words, as if half-asleep . . .

Very truly yours,
C. L. Dodgson

◆

*To Henry Savile Clarke*

THE CHESTNUTS, GUILDFORD
31 DECEMBER 1886

Dear Mr Savile Clarke,

I got a great deal of amusement and pleasure yesterday afternoon in seeing *Alice in Wonderland*. I think Phoebe *very good indeed*: and little Dorothy is a genius! I should like to have a long talk with you over the whole thing, and possibly might make a useful suggestion or two: but I hope you would feel *perfectly* free (and it won't wound my vanity a bit) to reject every suggestion I may make . . .

I am glad Mrs Savile Clarke liked the book.

Very truly yours,
C. L. Dodgson

*Sylvie and Bruno* was meant to interest adults as well as amuse children, and was set in no fewer than three parallel worlds, between which the narrator (clearly Dodgson himself) continually moves,

ABOVE: *Alice, played by Phoebe Carlo in the first stage production of 'Alice in Wonderland' (1886), with the Dormouse.*

RIGHT: *Alice and the Gryphon listening to the Mock Turtle's song, from 'Alice in Wonderland'. The operetta was written with Dodgson's agreement by Henry Savile Clarke. Dodgson had numerous thoughts on its staging, most of which Savile Clarke ignored.*

usually becoming invisible in the two other-worldy ones. First there is the real world, 'Society', in which a young doctor named Arthur becomes enamoured of Lady Muriel, and eventually wins her. Next there is 'Outland', in which the Sub-Warden and his wife plot to have their stupid and vicious son, Uggug, made their successor in place of the Warden's son, Bruno. Bruno and his sister, Sylvie, periodically take refuge in the third realm, 'Elfland', where they are fairies a few inches high, have a loving father, and make fairy gardens. Neither *Sylvie and Bruno*, nor its successor, *Sylvie and Bruno Concluded* (1893), had the success of the *Alice* books.

RIGHT: *'Words fail me to describe the beauty of the little group ... Sylvie reclining with her elbow buried in the moss, and her rosy cheek resting in the palm of her hand, and Bruno stretched at her feet with his head in her lap.'* Sylvie and Bruno. *Furniss used his own children as models.*

*By 1886 Dodgson was in regular correspondence with the artist Harry Furniss about illustrations for* Sylvie and Bruno. *Only one page of this letter survives.*

CHRIST CHURCH, OXFORD
11 NOVEMBER 1886

Dear Mr Furniss,

I have a very important request to make of you — in view of the following considerations:

(1) It is now just a year and 8 months since you undertook the illustrating of my new book, and only 4 pictures are as yet delivered: at which rate it would take more than 30 years to finish the book!

(2) It is most desirable to get the pictures drawn and the book published. Life is uncertain.

(3) I can undertake to keep you continuously employed from this time onwards, till it is done, even if you do as much as a picture a week.

(4) This job may fairly claim your special attention, being a tolerably big order!

(5) I notice that you are at present drawing for the *Illustrated London News*, as well as *Punch*. This must not only use up all your time, but also all your brain and hand powers.

My request is, then, that . . .

ABOVE: *Cartoon by Harry Furniss, Dodgson's illustrator for both his* Sylvie and Bruno *books, caricaturing himself (right) and Dodgson (left).*

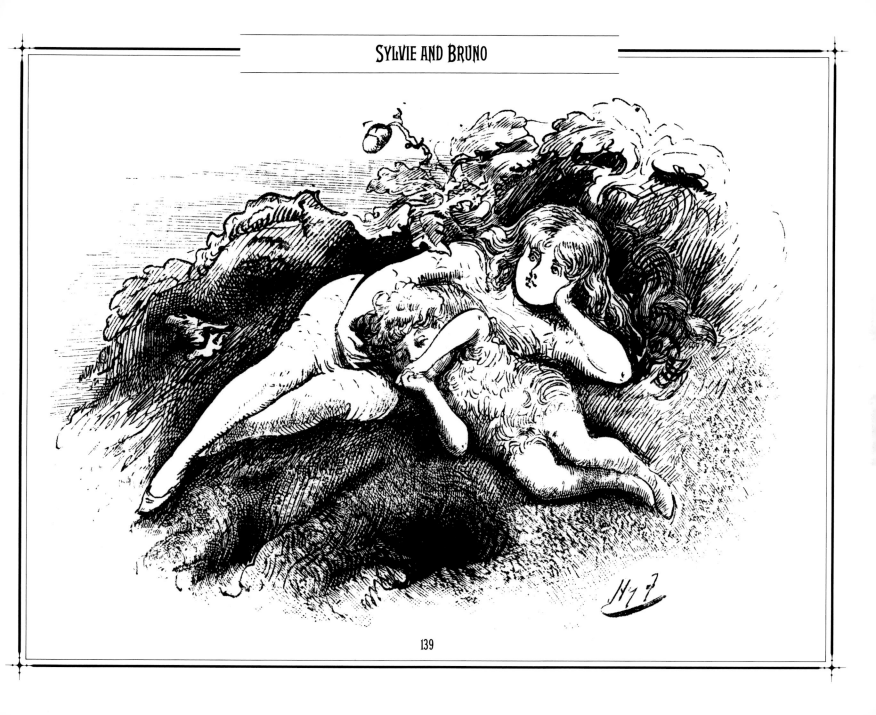

*He wrote again later in the month.*

CHRIST CHURCH, OXFORD
29 NOVEMBER 1886

Dear Mr Furniss,

... As to Sylvie, I am charmed with your idea of dressing her in *white*: it exactly fits my own idea of her: I want her to be a sort of embodiment of Purity. So I think that, in Society, she should be *wholly* in white — white frock ('clinging,' certainly: I *hate* the crinoline fashion): white stockings (or wouldn't socks be prettier? When children have, what is not always the case, well-shaped calves to their legs, stockings seem a pity): and I think white satin shoes would be better than black. Also I *think* we might venture on making her *fairy*-dress transparent. Don't you think we might face Mrs Grundy to *that* extent? In fact I think Mrs G. would be fairly content at finding her *dressed*, and would not mind whether the material was silk, or muslin, or even gauze.

If Sylvie is in white, oughtn't Bruno to be so also? But the *style* of his dress I find I can make nothing of: invention fails me.

One thing more. *Please* don't give Sylvie high heels! They are an abomination to me.

Very Truly yours,
C. L. Dodgson

*"NEVER!" yelled Tottles And he meant it.*

*31/8/87*

*Writing to Harry Furniss three years later, in November 1889, Dodgson was unduly pessimistic;* Sylvie and Bruno *was published before the end of the year.*

CHRIST CHURCH, OXFORD
1 NOVEMBER 1889

Dear Mr Furniss,

Let me congratulate you on having finished your 4-years' job! ... If only we could have reached our present point a month ago! However

LEFT AND RIGHT: *'See now this couple settled down:/In quiet lodgings, out of town:/Submissively the tearful wife/Accepts a plain and humble life:/Yet begs one boon on bended knee:/"My ducky-darling, don't resent it!/Mamma might come for two or three—"/ "NEVER!" yelled Tottles. And he meant it.' Dodgson's preliminary sketch (left) accompanying the last verse of the French Count's 'Tottles' song in* Sylvie and Bruno Concluded; *and Furniss's final version (right).*

there's no use crying over spilt milk. It was a good deal *my* doing in not keeping you better supplied with complete, and arranged, text. I haven't yet heard whether Macmillan advises to aim at middle of January, or Easter, for publication. I much prefer the former date myself, if only that life is uncertain, and I want very much to see it *out*. Besides, the sooner I can get this job off my hands, the sooner I can begin on Vol. II. So I am continuing to work at it 6 or 8 hours a day . . .

Very sincerely yours,
C. L. Dodgson

*Although Dodgson made new child-friends, he also continued to remember old ones. He had written to Edith 'Dolly' Blakemore since she was nine, and they continued to correspond well into the 1890s.*

### CHRIST CHURCH, OXFORD
### 27 JANUARY 1882

My dear Edith,

Many thanks for your letter, and painted crocus, and paper-rack. I am very sorry your father is no better: when the summer comes, I think it will be a good thing if you advise him (you know how much he depends on your advice) to come to Eastbourne. Then sometimes I shall have the pleasure of seeing you, with my opera-glass, at the other end of the beach: and I shall be able to say 'There's Edith: I can see *her*: but I shall go home again if she looks this way, for fear of her seeing *me*.' And what do you think I am going to have for my birthday treat? *A whole plum-pudding*! It is to be about the size for four people to eat: and I shall eat it in my room, *all by myself*! The doctor says he is 'afraid I shall be ill': but *I* simply say '*Nonsense*!'

Your Loving friend,
C. L. Dodgson

RIGHT: *Beaching lobster boats at Eastbourne, where Dodgson continued to spend most of his summer holidays. '"Will you walk a little faster?" said a whiting to a snail./"There's a porpoise close behind us, and he's treading on my tail./See how eagerly the lobsters and the turtles all advance!/They are waiting on the shingle—will you come and join the dance?"' The Song of the Mock Turtle, describing the 'Lobster Quadrille', from* Alice's Adventures in Wonderland.

LEFT: *Dodgson's sketch in a letter to Edith Blakemore (this page), in which he plans his birthday celebrations.*

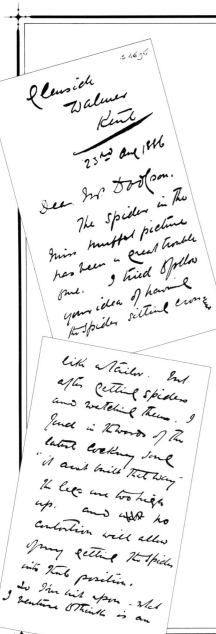

*To Edith Blakemore*

### CHRIST CHURCH, OXFORD
### 3 MARCH 1890

.. I *do* sympathise so heartily with you in what you say about feeling shy with children when you have to entertain them! Sometimes they are a real *terror* to me — especially boys: little girls I can now and then get on with, when they're few enough. They easily become *de trop*. But with little *boys* I'm out of my element altogether. I sent *Sylvie and Bruno* to an Oxford friend, and, in writing his thanks, he added, 'I think I must bring my little boy to see you.'

So I wrote to say '*don't*,' or words to that effect: and he wrote again that he could hardly believe his eyes when he got my note. He thought I doted on *all* children. But I'm *not* omnivorous! — like a pig. I pick and choose . . .

Your loving friend,
C. L. Dodgson

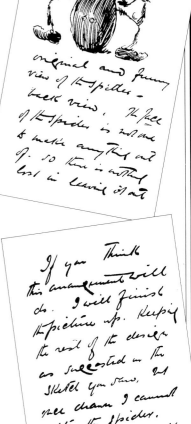

*Mrs Price's son, Frederick, had been a student with Dodgson at Christ Church.*

### CHRIST CHURCH, OXFORD
### 19 DECEMBER 1889

Dear Mrs Price,

One line in answer to the anxiety you so kindly express about my presumed 'delicacy of health.' It consists of the malady called 'being fifty-seven.' I've never known serious illness: that bout of ague, in which you so kindly nursed me, is one of the worst I have had.

But years go very quick at 57, and one cannot count on 10 or 20 years more of active life, with *quite* the gay confidence of a man of 27! . . .

Most truly yours,
C. L. Dodgson

LEFT: *Furniss's seven-year collaboration with Dodgson on the* Sylvie and Bruno *books generated a great deal of correspondence and not a small amount of ill-feeling (Furniss once threatened to end the partnership when Dodgson rejected two of his drawings). In this letter to Dodgson, he explained that he cannot make the spider sit cross-legged like a tailor because 'it ain't built that way.'*

LEFT: *'And his soul shall be sad for the Spider,/When Miss Muffet was sipping her whey,/That so tenderly sat down beside her,/And scared her away!' Furniss's final illustration of the spider (legs still uncrossed) for the Professor's song in* Sylvie and Bruno Concluded.

*In her reminiscences Enid Stevens wrote 'I don't think anybody else ever had so much of him as I had . . . I was the last child-friend.' Soon after Dodgson met her he wrote to her mother.*

### CHRIST CHURCH, OXFORD
#### 28 FEBRUARY 1891

Dear Mrs Stevens,

I have lost a considerable fraction (say .25) of my heart to your little daughter: and I *hope* you will allow me further opportunities of trying whether or no we can become real *friends*. She would be about my only child-friend — in Oxford. The former ones have grown up: and I've taken no trouble to find others, it's such a lottery, the finding of any *lovable* ones . . .

Sincerely yours,
C. L. Dodgson

LEFT: *'At this the whole pack rose up into the air, and came flying down upon her: she gave a little scream, half of fright and half of anger, and tried to beat them off, and found herself lying on the bank, with her head in the lap of her sister, who was gently brushing away some dead leaves that had fluttered down from the trees upon her face.'* Tenniel's illustration for Alice's Adventures in Wonderland, *later coloured for* The Nursery 'Alice'.

*To Enid Stevens*

### CHRIST CHURCH, OXFORD
#### 7 APRIL 1891

My DEAR Enid,

So you think you've got the courage to come a walk by yourself with me? Indeed! Well, I shall come for you on April 31st at 13 o'clock, and first I will take you to the Oxford Zoological Gardens, and put you into a cage of LIONS, and when they've had a good feed, I'll put whatever is left of you into a cage of TIGERS. Then I'll bring you to my rooms, and give a regular beating, with a thick stick, to my new little friend. Then I'll put you into the coal-hole, and feed you for a week on nothing but bread and water. Then I'll send you home in a milk-cart, in one of the empty milk-cans. And after that, if ever I come for you again, you'll scream louder than a COCKATOO!

Your Loving friend,
Lewis Carroll

### DIARY 17 APRIL (F) 1891

. . . I went as arranged to fetch Enid Stevens for walk and tea — first experiment at having her alone. She was with me from 3 to 6, a charming companion, and, what many children are *not*, able to *talk*.

*Dodgson continued to write to Enid Stevens for the rest of his life. On this occasion, she had to watch the intercollege boat races without him.*

### CHRIST CHURCH, OXFORD
#### 21 MAY 1897

My darling,

What is it you want? If it is, to go *with* you to see the Eights, I fear I must beg off. I can give you a small fraction of my love (say .0001 of a very hard heart), or I can give you a written request, which would secure the admission, to our Barge, of you and your mother and a

BELOW: *'She had never before seen a rabbit with either a waistcoat-pocket, or a watch to take out of it.'*
Alice's Adventures in Wonderland

gentleman-friend, if you like to take one with you — but I can't give you *time*!

Your very loving,
C. L. D.

P.S. What! A *High School girl* deficient in the *courage* needed to enter a set of College Rooms, even though the owner *is* a very slight acquaintance? Such a thing cannot be! Evidently you were thinking of a visit to a *dentist*, and got the two ideas mixed up together.

---

*This year Dodgson put his determination to keep his two personalities separate into print. He had a circular prepared to send to correspondents who wrote to him as Mr Dodgson to inquire about the works of Lewis Carroll.*

Mr Dodgson is so frequently addressed by strangers on the quite unauthorised assumption that he claims, or at any rate acknowledges the authorship of books not published under his name, that he has found it necessary to print this, once for all, as an answer to all such applications. He neither claims nor acknowledges any connection with any pseudonym, or with any book that is not published under his own name. Having therefore no claim to retain, or even to read the enclosed, he returns it for the convenience of the writer who has thus misaddressed it.

---

*In 1891, after thirty-six years as Dean of Christ Church, Liddell finally retired. Whatever ill-feeling Dodgson may have had at one time for Mrs Liddell seems now to have been forgotten.*

CHRIST CHURCH, OXFORD
12 NOVEMBER 1891

Dear Mrs Liddell,

. . . It is *very* hard to find words which seem to express, adequately, how strongly I feel the very *great* loss, to the University, the College, the City, and to myself, involved in the going away of the

Dean and yourself. We, as the Governing Body, have had a chief of such exceedingly rare qualities that it would be vain to hope that *any* successor can *quite* fill his place. I am sure that the whole of Oxford, and all the good and charitable work carried on in it, will suffer great and permanent loss by the absence of yourself. And, to *me*, life in Christ Church will be a totally different thing when the faces, familiar to me for 36 years, are seen no more among us. It seems but yesterday when the Dean, and you, first arrived: yet I was hardly more than a boy, then; and many of the pleasantest memories of those early years — that foolish time that seemed as if it would last for ever — are bound up with the names of yourself and your children: and now I am an old man, already beginning to feel a little weary of life — at any rate weary of its *pleasures*, and only caring to go on, on the chance of doing a little more *work* . . .

Sincerely and gratefully yours,<br>C. L. Dodgson

---

*Mrs Hargreaves was not able to accept the following invitation, but next day she did 'very kindly come over . . . for a short time'. (This was the last mention of Alice in his diary.)*

CHRIST CHURCH, OXFORD
8 DECEMBER 1891

My dear Mrs Hargreaves,

I should be glad if you could, quite conveniently to yourself, look in for tea any day. You would probably prefer to bring a companion; but I must leave the choice to you, only remarking that if your husband is here he would be most very welcome (I crossed out most because it's ambiguous; most words are, I fear). I met him in our Common Room not long ago. It was hard to realise that he was the husband of one I can scarcely picture to myself, even now, as more than 7 years old!

Always sincerely yours,<br>C. L. Dodgson

The Wonderland

Postage-Stamp Case

LEFT: *The "Wonderland" Postage-Stamp Case which Dodgson devised in 1888 and then had commercially manufactured. When the case was opened, the baby Alice was holding in her arms turned into a pig. The case had pockets for twelve stamps of varying values, and was issued with an accompanying pamphlet,* Eight or Nine Wise Words about Letter-Writing.

*E. Gertrude Thomson was now illustrating Dodgson's verse collection,* Three Sunsets and Other Poems, *first published in 1861.*

### CHRIST CHURCH, OXFORD
### 27 FEBRUARY 1893

My dear Miss Thomson,

. . . In the 'bower' picture, surely the elder child has the form of a *girl*? It is not an easy subject to discuss with a lady, but perhaps to a lady-*artist* I may mention, without offence, that the breasts are those of a girl, not a boy. To the best of my recollection, you have given them just the curvature which I noticed in the last child-model (Maud Howard, aged 14) whom I had the privilege of trying to copy in Mrs Shute's studio. If you would add to the hair, and slightly refine the wrist and ankles, it would make a beautiful girl. I had much rather have *all* the fairies *girls*, if you wouldn't mind. For I confess I do *not*

RIGHT: *Montage for the lid of the "Looking-Glass" Biscuit-Tin . Dodgson had sanctioned the production of the tin, but would have preferred it to have been sold empty, rather than full of biscuits which he did not 'have any wish for'.*

HUMPTY DUMPTY *
OFFERING HIS HAND
TO ALICE

THE WHITE KNIGHT
Sliding Down The
POKER.

admire naked *boys* in pictures. They always seem to me to need *clothes*: whereas one hardly sees why the lovely forms of girls should *ever* be covered up!

If ever you fancy any of the pictures look too like real *children*, then by all means give them wings . . .

Very sincerely yours,
C. L. Dodgson

---

*Harry Furniss was now completing the illustrations for* Sylvie and Bruno Concluded.

7 LUSHINGTON ROAD, EASTBOURNE
21 OCTOBER 1893

Dear Mr Furniss,

On further examination, with a magnifying-glass, of this drawing, I find that Bruno *has* a waist. *Without* the glass, the effect is, distinctly, that his right side is bounded by the line of light that runs down the front of Sylvie's skirt, and thus that he is in a loose sort of shirt. Yet there is a piece of window-sill between the 2 figures, which (if it were as much illuminated as the portion to the left-hand of Bruno) would clearly show where Bruno's figure ended. But this bit, for some inexplicable reason, you have shaded. *What* is supposed to cast a shadow on it?

I must really *beg* you to make *both* dresses more opaque. If you look through a magnifying-glass, you will see that the 'hind-quarters' still show very plainly through: in fact, this is quite visible, even *without* a glass . . .

Very sincerely yours,
C. L. Dodgson

---

DIARY 24 DEC (Sun) 1893

First sight of a complete *Sylvie and Bruno Concluded*. A dozen arrived from Macmillan.

### DIARY 27 DEC (W) 1893

To town, and spent some hours at Macmillans', writing in copies of *Sylvie and Bruno Concluded.*

LEFT AND RIGHT: *Furniss's illustration for the final page (left) and frontispiece (right) of* Sylvie and Bruno Concluded. *The book was dedicated to Enid Stevens (who claimed to have been the last child-friend Dodgson made) in the form of an acrostic that spelt her name with the third letter of each line.*

*Dodgson had first met Mary Brown at Whitby (weeping, her stocking torn) when she was nine. She was now twenty-two.*

### 7 LUSHINGTON ROAD, EASTBOURNE
### 21 AUGUST 1894

My dear Mary,

I wonder if you have an idea what sort of thing it is to have with you, every day (for I bring it with me here from Oxford), a bundle of unanswered letters, the oldest more than 5½ years old! The very sight of it suggests, 'You've many an hour of steady work before you, before I shall be got rid of!' and then one is apt to think 'work that has waited so many *years* can easily wait another day!' The temptation to procrastinate, with such formidable arrears on hand, is almost irresistible!

Your loving old friend,
Charles L. Dodgson

*Stuart Collingwood was Dodgson's nephew and first biographer.*

### CHRIST CHURCH, OXFORD
### 12 FEBRUARY 1896

My dear Stuart,

It seems a very good idea of yours, to try to earn something with your pen, though I fear you will find that the line of 'reviewing' is, like every other line, very crowded. The best thing I can think of, to help you, would be for you to choose some recent book, and to write a review of it, just as you would if it were going to be published, and send me the MS, which I would submit to a friend, an experienced editor, and would get you a thoroughly reliable opinion as to whether

LEFT: *Portrait of Charles Dodgson painted shortly after his death. Despite his sober University robes, his expression betrays something of the playful wit that delighted in the pursuit of the ridiculous and the nonsensical.*

'there's money in it' or not. If he encourages you, I could probably learn from him what sort of pay your work would be likely to get.

Your affectionate uncle,
Charles L. Dodgson

*On 5 January 1898 Dodgson, in bed with bronchitis, wrote the three letters which were probably his last. The bronchitis became pneumonia and he died on 14 January 1898. His advice about funerals is with regard to the recent death of Stuart Collingwood's father.*

THE CHESTNUTS, GUILDFORD
5 JANUARY 1898

My dear Stuart,

I have sent you a message, of love and sympathy, through your mother. This note is on a business-matter that will not wait.

When my dear Father died in 1868, we gave almost *carte blanche* to the undertakers, without any stipulations as to *limit* of expense. The consequence was a *gigantic* bill — so large, that we had great difficulty in getting the authorities at Doctors' Commons to sanction such extravagance. If I had the thing to do again, I should say to the undertaker 'Now that you know *all* that is required, I wish you to give me a signed promise that your charges *shall not exceed a stipulated sum*.' I should then take the advice of experienced friends as to whether the limit named was a reasonable one; and, if they said 'no,' I should apply to another undertaker.

You and your mother will have to live with the strictest economy: you have no money to throw away.

Your affectionate uncle,
Charles L. Dodgson

ABOVE: *All his life, Dodgson guarded his privacy carefully and tried to keep his two identities separate. Very rarely did he sign a letter 'Lewis Carroll', and then only to the young friends who shared his fantasy world.*

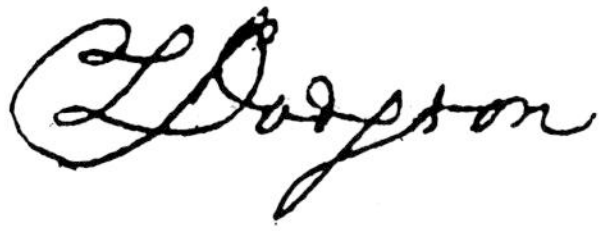

| | |
|---|---|
| 1832 | Born (27 January), the eldest son (third of eleven children) of Charles Dodgson, Perpetual Curate of Daresbury, Cheshire, and Frances Jane (born Lutwidge). |
| 1843 | Father became Rector of Croft, Yorkshire, and family moved there. |
| 1844–5 | At Richmond School, Yorkshire (from 1 August 1844). |
| 1844–9 | Wrote a series of magazines to entertain his family: *Useful and Instructive Poetry, The Rectory Magazine, The Comet, The Rosebud, The Star, The Will-O-the-Wisp* and *The Rectory Umbrella*. |
| 1846–9 | At Rugby School (from 27 January 1846). |
| 1850 | Matriculated at Christ Church, Oxford (23 May). |
| 1851 | Took up residence at Christ Church (24 January). Mother died (26 January). |
| 1852 | Student of Christ Church (December 1852, until his death). |
| 1854 | B.A. (1st Class Honours in Mathematics; 2nd Class in Classics). |
| 1855 | Sub-Librarian, Christ Church (until 1857). Mathematical Lecturer (until 1881). Compiled *Mischmasch*, a scrapbook of his best writings. |
| 1856 | First met Liddell family (February). Bought his first camera (March). First photographed Alice Liddell (April). |
| 1857 | M.A. |
| 1861 | Ordained deacon (22 December). |
| 1862 | Told the story of Alice's adventures to the Liddell sisters on a boat trip (4 July). |
| 1865 | *Alice's Adventures in Wonderland* published (July); reprinted at Tenniel's request, due to poor picture quality (November). |
| 1867 | Journey on the Continent with H. P. Liddon (13 July–14 September). |
| 1868 | Father died (21 June). Moved his family to Guildford (1 September). |
| 1871 | *Through the Looking-Glass and What Alice Found There* published (December). |
| 1876 | *The Hunting of the Snark* published (March). |
| 1877 | First took Eastbourne summer lodgings (31 July). |
| 1881 | Resigned Mathematical Lectureship (but retained his Studentship) to devote more time to writing. |
| 1882 | Curator of Senior Common Room, Christ Church (December 1882 to February 1892). |
| 1886 | *Alice's Adventures Under Ground* (original MS version of *Alice's Adventures in Wonderland* given to Alice Liddell) published. 'Alice in Wonderland', an operetta based on both the *Alice* books, first performed. |
| 1889 | *Sylvie and Bruno* published. |
| 1890 | *The Nursery 'Alice'* published. |
| 1892 | Resigned Curatorship of Senior Common Room, Christ Church (February). |
| 1893 | *Sylvie and Bruno Concluded* published. |
| 1898 | Died at Guildford (14 January) and buried there. *Three Sunsets and Other Poems* published. |

# ACKNOWLEDGEMENTS

*The illustrations are reproduced by kind permission of the following:*
Ashmolean Museum, Oxford: 122. Bridgeman Art Library, London: 27, 82, 83, and with acknowledgement to Bradford Art Galleries and Museums 39; Guildford House Gallery 78; Guildhall Art Galleries, City of London 87; Guildhall Library 38; Oscar and Peter Johnson Ltd, London 22; Maidstone Museum and Art Gallery, Kent 19; Transport Museum, York 75; Warrington Museum and Art Gallery 67; Wolverhampton Art Gallery, Staffordshire 98; Christopher Wood Gallery, London 90. The Governing Body, Christ Church, Oxford: 47, 150, 151, 154, and with acknowledgement to Mrs M. J. St Clair 24, 33, 40 left, 52 right, 80, 133 right, 134 left. Christie's London: 58, 59, 60, 61. Fine Art Photographic Library, London: 43, 50, 91, 110, 143. Guildford Muniment Room, Surrey County Council: 8, 10, 11, 17, 26, 76, 81, 100, 108. Harvard University, Houghton Library: 13 left, 74 right. Hulton-Deutsch, London: 52 left. Indiana University, Lilly Library: 124, 140. Mander and Mitchenson Theatre Collection, London: 126, 134–5, 136, 137. Mansell Collection, London: 25, 30, 31, 36, 37, 101, 125, 127, 131. National Gallery, London: 62 left. National Museum of Photography, Film and Television, Bradford: 12, 28, 41, 92 left. National Portrait Gallery, London: 7, 23, 35, 44, 48, 65, 68, 88, 92 right, 120, 138. New York Public Library, Henry W. and Albert A. Berg Collection: 105, 129. New York University, Alfred C. Berol Collection: 40 right, 109, 142. Art Gallery of Ontario, Toronto: 118. Oxfordshire County Libraries, The Local Studies Collection, Central Library: 32, 53, 148–9. Princeton University Library, New York: 13 right, 107. Rosenbach Museum and Library, Philadelphia: 115, 123. The Marquis of Salisbury: 106–7. The University of Texas at Austin, Harry Ransom Humanities Research Centre: 29 right, 57 right, 74 left, 104, 114, 117. Thomas-Photos, Oxford: 70 left. © The Board of Trustees of the Victoria and Albert Museum, London: 116.

*These illustrations come from the following books:*
Lewis Carroll, *The Nursery 'Alice'*, 1890: Frontispiece, 51, 62 right, 71, 130 right, 134, 146, 147; *Alice's Adventures Underground*, 1886 (facsimile of original manuscript): 54–5, 56–7, 119, 130 left, 133 left. Morton N. Cohen, *The Letters of Lewis Carroll*, 1979, Vol. I, Macmillan London Ltd: 16, 54 right. Stuart Dodgson Collingwood, *The Lewis Carroll Picture Book*, 1899: 20–21; *The Life and Letters of Lewis Carroll*, 1898: half-title, 9, 14, 15, 34, 72, 86 left, 144. Evelyn M. Hatch, *A Selection of the Letters of Lewis Carroll to His Child-Friends*, 1933: 93, 128. James Ingram, *Memorials of Oxford*, 1832–7: 28–9. S. H. Williams and F. Madan, *A Handbook of Literature of the Rev. C. L. Dodgson*, 1931: 63.